Pen'd in His Presence.

Come closer. Listen in.
He's been waiting to meet you here.

By: Melanie Nyanu

Scan the QR Code below to visit my website for a surprise

& for information on how to connect with me

-xoxo, Melanie.

ISBN: 979-8-9936453-0-8

Dedication

For those learning to hear God,
to write what they cannot yet say,
and to surrender before they fully understand,
this book is for you.

For the seekers. For the scribes.
For the ones still searching.
For those who scribble and whisper prayers between tears.
For every heart daring to come undone in His presence,
this book was written with you in mind.

To the community of hearts who long for more.
more of His voice, His nearness, His truth,
who crave more of Him and less of everything else,
may your seeking never cease.
May you never settle for distance from Him.

And to those yet to read these words,
may generation after generation
live with hearts awakened to His nearness,
and may you never stop seeking His presence.

— Xoxo, Melanie ♥

Unto Him

My ever-present Answer, my Lord, my Savior,
my Father, my Teacher, my Friend...

May every word in these pages point back to You.
Not to me, but to Your Holy presence that never fades,
to Your unfailing love that reaches beyond my understanding.
May every line bring You glory,
reflecting the depths of Your love and mercy,
the heights of Your grace, and the vastness of Your faithfulness.

Thank You, for the immeasurable privilege of being Your
instrument. Thank You for choosing to write through my doubts
and fears, and through the broken places I never thought could
be used. Thank You for Your patience with me. I am humbled
beyond measure that You would trust me to carry even a whisper
of Your voice. This is not my work, it is Yours alone.

Every word is a gift from You.
All glory, all honor, and praise belong to You forever.
I love you ♥

Pen'd in His Presence is more than a book, it is an invitation into the place where He speaks. These words are not neat or rehearsed. They are more like messy handwriting, tear-stained journal pages, and honest scribbles in the margins of my Bible. They are unfiltered, unfinished, unguarded thoughts of a heart still learning to trust Him. These pages are fragments of His presence. Small, undeniable pieces of Himself scattered through ordinary days, quiet prayers, honest tears, and intimate moments in the safety of my secret place. These fragments are not the whole picture, but they are evidence enough to remind us that He is always present and always speaking.

It was my pen that traced His voice through the cracks of my doubt and unbelief. With every stroke, the walls I hid behind collapsed. My pride unraveled, my fears exposed, my idols torn down. My false sense of security and illusion of control, all stripped away, like words hidden beneath white-out, making room for truth to be written instead. These pages carry the weight of worship, the courage of honesty, the quiet strength of surrender, the ache of longing, the hope of deliverance, and the covering of grace that holds it all together.

This book is for the one desperate to hear His voice again, as well as for the one trying to recognize it for the first time. These words were pen'd in the stillness, in the wrestle, in the wonder, in

His presence. And may they serve as an invitation to come close, listen in, and let Him speak... He's been waiting to meet you here.

The red text pen'd throughout these pages reflect the words I believe God spoke to my heart. Not to exalt my interpretation, but as a simple, reverent, and familiar way to honor His voice. I offer them here not as perfect transcripts, but as fragments of His presence, knowing they are only part of the conversation... the rest is yours to have with Him.

" Thus says the Lord...Write in a book all the words that I have spoken to you." [- Jeremiah 30:2]

I Have Seen the Lord

Lord, I praise You because I am not defined by my past.

Not by the darkness I once walked in, not by the idols I bowed to, not by the deception that clouded my vision. Witchcraft, false gods, and broken altars once marked my story. They grieved me so deeply that shame tried to silence me and fear tried to paralyze me. The enemy whispered, "You're unworthy to speak for Him. Too defiled to be His instrument." But God, just like You did for Mary Magdalene, You stepped into my hell and pulled me out.

You didn't just rescue me. You redeemed me.

You refined me. You called me.

While I thought I was being led to destruction,

You were grooming my loyalty, shaping my discipline, preparing my surrender. You saw me in the depths, and You came.

You wrapped me in mercy and called me Your own.

And now, even as I stand in the light, I confess the fear, the doubt, the unbelief that still whispers: "Can He really use me?"

But today I silence that lie in the name of Jesus.

Because the cross says YES.

Yes, You can use me.

Yes, You have called me to write, to speak, to teach and to declare Your truth. Not in my strength but in Your Spirit.

I am not disqualified, I am redeemed.

I don't speak from theory, I speak from encounter.

I write not from religious duty, but from redemption's fire.

I am not here by accident, You have sent me to proclaim what You have done and what You are still doing.

Like Mary outside the tomb, I declare:

"I have seen the Lord!"[1]

I've seen You in my healing.

I've seen You in the undoing of lies and the rebuilding of my soul.

I've seen You take what was meant for evil and use it to plant something sacred.

This is my commissioning.

Like Mary, I carry a testimony the world needs to hear.

Not polished, but powerful.

Not perfect, but anointed.

So Father, I yield again.

Take this life. Take these hands. Take this voice.

Let it all echo Your glory and testify of a God who rescues, redeems, and reigns forever.

I have seen the Lord.

And because I have, I cannot stay silent.

---

[1] John 20:18

Dayenu [It would have been enough][2]

If God had simply saw me in my brokenness,
When I was lost and without hope,
And told me I was not alone,
It would have been enough.

If God had pulled me from the cycle of addiction,
And freed me from generational cycles,
It would have been enough.

If God had forgiven my past sins,
And showed me grace where I had failed,
It would have been enough.

If God had filled me with His presence,
And transformed my heart to love as He loves,
It would have been enough.

If God had made me whole again,
Restored my soul, and given me new purpose,

---

[2] Dayenu: Jewish tradition to express gratefulness for Gods acts, recognizing that even one act alone would have been enough to praise Him, yet He kept doing more.

It would have been enough.

If God had shown me that He loves me,
Not because of what I've done, but because of who He is,
It would have been enough.

If God had simply given me His Word,
And guided me through the lies of the enemy,
It would have been enough.

But God did not stop there...
He continues to work in my life,
Guiding me, loving me,
And calling me to serve Him,
Sharing my testimony as proof of His love,
That others may see and believe,
It will never be enough to express His goodness.

Thank You, God, for all that You have done.
I love you and honor you.
In Jesus name, Amen.

Made for His presence.

God, I just want to be in Your presence reading, learning, sitting with You. But I often feel like I have to choose between You and life's responsibilities. I'm not tired like I need a nap. I'm tired because I need You. I need time with You. It feels like the time I need in Your presence is increasing, like my spirit is hungrier than it used to be. God, I feel like I need a new rhythm. I can tell when I haven't been with You. I'm more like me and less like You. More fleshy. More emotional. More impatient. My pride rises up. Do I need to fast? I just know I need to be with You. What's the minimum amount of time I need to spend with you Lord? What's the daily amount I should wrestle for? Teach me to practice Your presence even when I can't run to my secret place.

I've been waiting for this moment with you. You never have to choose between Me and your responsibilities. I want to be in all of it.[3] I AM not only in the quiet places; I walk with you in the busy ones too. Let Me in. Let Me meet you in the dishes, in the car, in the meetings and the mundane moments. I AM not asking for performance. I AM longing for connection.

I know the weight you carry, and I know your heart wants Me more than anything. That desire, that ache you feel, that's Me drawing you nearer to Me. You don't need to earn My presence; you

---

[3] Psalm 139:7-10

just need to turn toward Me. Yes, there will be times I call you away to fast, to rest, to be still. But more than that, I want to teach you to abide. Your minimum is not a number, it's a rhythm. It is a heartbeat that says, Here I AM, Lord. I want You.

You were made for My presence, and I'm drawing you deeper into it. I AM the one stirring that hunger in you. Not to overwhelm you, but to sustain you. You feel more like "you" because you've tasted what it's like to be more like Me. That pull you feel is My grace calling you back. You don't need to measure your time with Me like a checklist. I want you to learn to abide. The whispered "Jesus, I need You," even while your hands are full. Your minimum is not a number— it's a posture. [4]

[4] Matthew 11:28-30

All I Want is You

God, I say You are all I need but sometimes my life tells a different story. I run to things that feel safe, even when I know they can't save me. I don't want to love anything more than I love You. I don't want to build my life around fragile things that will one day fall apart and disappear. But the truth is, sometimes it feels easier to trust what I can see, touch, and control. I don't want to live that way anymore. I don't want to bow to fear, approval, success, comfort, or anything else that promises life but only leaves me emptier. I want You to be the only One I trust. The only One I worship. Please, God, reveal the places where my hands and my heart are still clutching idols. Teach me to loosen my grip. Tear down the false gods I've built my hope on and build Your throne in their place.

I don't just want parts of You, I want all of You.

And I want You to have all of me.

Show me where I've made comfort into a counterfeit place of refuge.

Show me where I've made success into my source of identity.

Show me where I've made people's approval into my foundation.

Show me where I've made fear into a master over me.

Show me where I've made control into an illusion of safety.

Show me where I've made Your gifts into my gods.

Show me where I've made my own plans into my security.

Show me where I've made routine into religion.

Show me where I've turned striving into worship.
Show me where I've made comfort into a cage.
Show me where I've clung to control instead of trusting You.
I don't want anything on the throne of my heart but You.

I see you. I see the war inside you.
The pull toward what feels safe and the ache for what is real.
You don't have to free yourself.[5]
I AM the One who gently loosens your grip and leads you into freedom.
I know why you ran to those idols.
They promised you something immediate when your heart was tired of waiting. But I offer you something deeper — Myself.
I AM not angry with your struggle; I AM compassionate toward it.[6]
I AM not impatient with your weakness; I draw near to it.[7]
You don't have to be perfect to come back to Me — just willing.
Let Me be the One who tears down what cannot hold you.
Let Me build what is unshakable within you.
Your idols are no match for My love.[8]

---

[5] John 8:36

[6] Psalm 103:13

[7] 2 Corinthians 12:9

[8] Romans 8:38-39

Let Me rewire your instincts, heal your fears, and teach you the joy of trust.
Even when your fingers slip back to old comforts, I AM still holding you. I AM pulling you closer.
I AM setting your heart free.
Your heart is mine.

Pressure Reveals What's Hidden

[As I power washed the fences]

God, do you see how dirty these fences are? As the power washer hits it, you can really see how the layers of dirt that had built up over time start to wash away. On the surface, it didn't seem that dirty, but once the pressure was on, I realized just how much was hiding underneath.

That's how it is with your heart too. When I draw you close and apply pressure through trials, truth, and conviction I reveal what's buried deep down. It might be painful, but it's necessary. You may not even realize what you're holding onto: fear, pride, bitterness, things that seem small but block the freedom I want for you.

Yeah, I noticed that the more I got closer with the power washer, the deeper things started to rise. It wasn't just surface dirt anymore. It was all the stuff that had settled in over time, stuff I thought I had dealt with but didn't know was still there.

That's the beauty of the process. The closer you come to Me, the more the hidden things surface. The pressure might feel uncomfortable, but it's a sign that I AM at work. It's not about punishing you, but about cleaning what's been hidden. The pressure isn't meant to harm you, it's meant to purify you, to get you closer to who I have made you to be. What's uncomfortable now is the process of letting go, but it's the only way to experience real freedom. What rises to the surface, I will cleanse. What you thought was a part of you, I will refine. Trust the pressure—it's My love at work. Let Me do the deep cleaning.

okay, fine. I'll trust You. I'll let go of the things I've been holding on to and let You clean me up.

That's it. Keep coming close, the pressure is just part of the process. You're becoming who I've always intended you to be.[9]

_____

[9] Corinthians 4:8-9

...even in the silence?

God, why are You not talking to me? Why can't I hear You? It feels like You are so far away. Are you upset with me? Did I do something wrong?

My silence is not punishment. My silence is preparation. I understand that it feels uncomfortable, but it's in this silence that I am doing a deeper work in you. You see, silence doesn't mean that I am absent. In fact, I am closer to you than you realize, working in ways you can't yet see. Silence is an invitation to trust Me deeper, to rely on Me in a way that isn't based on what you can hear or feel. It's where I want you to choose to believe without seeing and to trust without hearing. This is where your faith is truly evaluated. I am creating in you a faith that will survive the silence and thrive even when you don't hear My voice as clearly. Just because you don't hear Me as clearly doesn't mean I've left you or abandoned you. If I promised something, I will come through. Trust that I am faithful, even in the quiet.[10] I am always at work, even when it seems like nothing is happening. Your faith is being shaped in ways you can't see yet. My silence isn't the end–it's a space where I am strengthening your trust in Me. Silence does not mean absence. I am NEVER absent.[11] Even

---

[10] 2 Corinthians 5:7

[11] Deuteronomy 31:6

when you can't hear Me in the way you expect, I am still here, guiding, moving, and working in your life. This is a season of deepening trust. I'm inviting you to lean on Me in a new way, to let go of what you think you need, and simply trust that I AM with you.[12] My presence is not defined by noise or what you hear. I am creating a faith in you that will endure beyond this moment. When I break the silence, you will see that I've been with you all along, even in the quiet.

_____

[12] Isaiah 41:10

Psalm of Praise

Lord, Thank You that You are Faithful.

Thank you for:

- Peace I didn't expect.
- Joy I didn't earn.
- Grace that never lets me go.
- Mercy that meets me in the middle of my mess.
- Strength when I have nothing left to give.
- Provision that comes right on time.
- Healing in places I didn't know were broken.
- Answers I didn't know I needed.
- Doors I couldn't open-opened by Your hand.
- Doors I couldn't close- closed by Your hand.
- Battles I didn't fight—won by Your power.
- Comfort in the silence.
- Favor I couldn't explain.
- Love that chased me down.
- Forgiveness that rewrote my story.
- Redemption that gave new meaning to my scars.
- Purpose in every detour.
- Hope that whispered louder than my fear.
-

I'm standing in the evidence of a faithful God.
Not because I have it all together.
Not because I've always been faithful.

Not because I've never doubted,

Not because I've always chosen right.

Not because I deserved it.

But because You are faithful.

From Striving to Surrender

God, sometimes I don't even realize how tightly I'm holding on. I say I trust You, but then I still find myself trying to manage everything on my own. Even though I know You are faithful, my heart still braces itself, anticipating disappointment. I get stuck in this exhausting cycle of striving, pushing, and wearing myself out. I want to trust You more, but honestly, I'm scared. What if I let go and everything falls apart? Letting go feels so vulnerable. I don't even know how to begin loosening my grip. Please teach me, Lord. I want to trust You with the things I can't control. Help me rest in You instead of striving. Help me lean on You instead of relying on my own strength. Remind me, moment by moment, that I was never meant to carry this alone. Grow my trust in You each day.

You learned self-reliance because you believed you had to survive on your own. But I AM not like those who failed you. I AM faithful and true. I never asked you to carry everything. I invited you to come to Me and find rest. What you release into My hands is never lost; it is made secure.

Your strength was never meant to come from within yourself, but from Me. Vulnerability with Me is not weakness, it is the door to real strength.

Let Me father you. Let Me defend you. Let Me provide for you.

Bring Me your worries one by one. Ask for My help in even the smallest things and I will guide you step by step. You were never meant to walk alone. I AM with you, always. [13]

---

[13] Psalm 55:22

Fear Must Bow

Lord, I can't. I am afraid.

Fear cannot stand in My presence. It doesn't matter how intimidating or overwhelming it seems—when I step in, fear has no choice but to bow.

The enemy may try to paralyze you with anxiety, doubt, and intimidation, but fear is powerless in My presence. Where My Spirit is, there is freedom.[14] Freedom from fear, freedom from torment, freedom from every lie that tries to grip your mind and heart. Fear is not your portion; it has already been defeated by the blood of Jesus.[15] I did not give you a spirit of fear, but of power, love, and a sound mind.[16] When I show up, fear trembles. Just as darkness flees when you turn on a light, fear must flee when My presence fills your life.[17] Stop giving fear permission to dictate your thoughts, your actions, or your destiny. It doesn't belong to you. It must bow.

I will not live in fear! I will not be held captive by anxiety or doubt! I stand in the authority of Jesus Christ, knowing that fear has no power over me. The King of Glory resides within me,

---

[14] Psalm 34:4

[15] Colossians 1:13-14

[16] 2 Timothy 1:7

[17] John 1:5

and where He is, fear must bow. Fear, you are not welcome here. You have no authority over my life, my mind, my family, or my future. I belong to God, and His perfect love casts out all fear. I will walk boldly, speak confidently, and live freely because God's presence surrounds me. Fear you will not have the final word. Jesus has already declared victory over you.

Psalm of Surrender

Oh Lord, I come to You,

Weary from striving, burdened by control.

I lay down my plans.

Remind me that I don't have to have it all figured out.

Guide me when I feel lost.

Calm me when I feel overwhelmed.

When things don't go the way I expect.

Help me to trust that You are still in control.

Teach me to let go of my own agenda and to follow Your lead instead.

Teach me to trust the paths You choose. I surrender my need to be in control. I surrender my doubts and my unbelief.

Take my life and see it in ways I can't even imagine.

Take my desires, reshape my heart until it beats in rhythm with Yours.

Take my hands, my voice, my mind, and let them serve you.

For You are eternal, the King of Kings and Lord of Lords.

So here I am, Lord, all I am, your instrument of revelation.

Use me, mold me, guide me.

In surrender, my heart is stilled.

Faith for the Unknown

God, it feels scary sometimes to step into places I don't know.
What if I'm not ready? What if I don't have what I need?
What if I get it wrong? What if I can't handle what's ahead?
It's easier to stay where I feel safe, where I can predict,
control, and prepare. But I hear You calling me deeper-out of
comfort and into trust. I don't want to miss what You have for
me because I was too afraid to move. I want to believe that if
You are leading me, You are also equipping me.
I just need to follow You, one faithful step at a time.
Strengthen my heart when I feel small. Steady my spirit when I
feel unsure. Help me move forward, not because I am fearless,
but because I am Yours.

I'm the one sending you. Where I send you, I have already gone
ahead of you. I've already prepared the way. What looks unknown
to you is fully known to Me.[18] Everything you will need is already
waiting for you there. Trust Me.[19] Provision may not always look
how you expect. Sometimes it will come as strength you didn't know
you had, people you didn't know you needed, doors you couldn't open
yourself, and growth you couldn't have produced on your own. I
supply it all. But much of it, you will only see as you move forward.
The manna falls when you step out. The water's part when you

---

[18] Deuteronomy 31:8
[19] Proverbs 3:5-6

walk into them. You don't have to figure out every detail. You don't have to be strong enough on your own. You only need to bring your trust. Bring your yes. I will bring the rest. Stay close to Me. Listen for My voice[20] in the stillness and in the steps.[21] I am not just sending you; I am going with you. I am your Guide, your Provider, your Defender, your Companion. You will never step into a place where I am not already present. You will never face a need I cannot meet. You will never fight a battle I have not already overcome. Do not be afraid of the unknown. The unknown to you is the known and prepared path to Me. Watch what I will do through your obedience.

I am with you — always.

---

[20] Isaiah 30:21

[21] Psalm 32:8

Freedom Beyond the Walls

God, I always thought that growth would only come through pain, heartbreak, and suffering. I always thought that I had to be shattered, crushed, in order to change. But You showed me something different. It wasn't my heart that needed to break into a thousand pieces this time; it was the walls I had built around it. The walls I thought were protecting me, but they were really my prison. I didn't even realize how small and heavy life had become inside those walls until You began to gently tear them down. You weren't trying to destroy me, You were trying to set me free.

I never meant for you to live caged.
Those walls kept out pain, yes but they also kept out joy, freedom, love, and My presence. I didn't come to break you; I came to free you.[22]

When My light touched your face, that's when true growth began.[23]
It wasn't destruction, it was awakening.
It was not devastation, it was liberation.
And now, without those walls, you are becoming everything I dreamed for you to be. This is what freedom feels like and it's only just beginning.

---

[22] Galatians 5:1

[23] 2 Corinthians 3:17

Window Seat

Whenever I fly, I always choose the window seat...
longing for that feeling of being close to God.
A brief moment where I release control.
In that stillness, I imagine the clouds as pillows resting in God's
lap, the sunlight brushing my face like a parent's gentle hand like
the scene in the movie *Selena*, when her mother ran her fingers
through her hair, offering comfort beyond words.

Up there, in that sacred space between earth and heaven,
I remember what it feels like to be small and safe at the same
time.
Just as that peace begins to settle in, sudden turbulence shakes
me, reminding me how rocky life can be. But I look back out the
window, into the distance, and find assurance again...
God is with me still,
not only here on this plane, but everywhere.
Always.

Never Hidden, Always Here

The clouds came and went, shifting in all shapes and sizes.
But through it all, the sun stood the same –
constant, unyielding, a quiet reminder that no matter how the
world shifts, there is One who remains unchanged.

Just as the clouds pass, so do our struggles, doubts, and storms.
But the Son remains –
steadfast, faithful, shining through it all, never wavering.

Chasing fireflies

God, seeking you in this world can sometimes feel like chasing fireflies, running after the quick light in the longer moments of darkness.

Trying to grasp it and hold on to it longer.

Gloves Off

God, I long for a safe space, a place where I can finally put the gloves down. I've been fighting battles, protecting myself, bracing for impact. But I don't want to live in defense anymore. I'm tired of the constant fight. I am tired of holding up walls that keep me from truly living.
Help me find that peace where I can let go.

I see your weary heart, and I'm here to offer you that safe space you long for. You don't have to keep fighting alone.
I will be your refuge.[24]
The place where you can lay down your guard and find rest.
In My presence, you can be vulnerable.
I am here to cover you, to hold you, to protect you, to defend you, to remind you that you're not in this alone.
But know this: peace comes through obedience, not avoidance.
The gloves must come down, not in weakness, but in trust.
I've already fought the greatest battle for you, and you are safe in Me. You also don't need to protect yourself from My discipline or correction because that's how I shape you. I don't call you to a life of self-defense, but to a life of surrender. Let go of control and remember what I've said: Be still, and know that I am God [25] When you trust Me fully, you will find rest. However,

---

[24] Psalm 91:1-2

[25] Psalm 46:10

you will need to lay down your pride and your need to fight on your own. Trust in My care, and the peace you seek will be yours.

Bound by Blindness

Many are asleep, untaught, and bound by idolatry. They are deceived, walking in a false sense of freedom, unaware of the bondage they are in. This blindness comes from a lack of biblical insight and true awareness of both themselves and My character. They are trapped by their fallen nature, and they don't realize the chains they've willingly accepted.[26] This kind of bondage is not the work of My Spirit; it is carnal bondage – the work of the flesh, sin, and the devil. People are living under the influence of sin, following the customs of the world, and being driven by fear of man. None of this is true freedom. They may think they are free, but they are enslaved to a lie.[27] Freedom in Me comes through surrender, through walking in the truth of My Word. The world offers counterfeit freedom, but it is empty. To truly experience the liberty I give, you must first recognize the bondage of sin and the flesh. Only then can you embrace the true freedom that is found in Christ alone.[28]

---

[26] Ephesians 4:18

[27] 2 Corinthians 4:4

[28] John 8:31-32

The Loosening

As you tend to your plants, you see glimpses of My heart for you. Just as you prune away the dead and overgrown parts of your plants, I, too, lovingly prune and remove what hinders you. Every cut, every trimming, is necessary for shaping you, for preparing you to bear greater fruit. It is not a punishment, but a process of refinement, a process that brings you closer to the fullness of what I have created you to be.

When you carefully loosen the roots of a plant, preparing it for a new environment, remember this: just as roots can become bound and stifled when confined, so too can your heart. Fear, sin, comfort zones, these things bind you, keeping you from growing as I intended. But when I loosen you, when I remove the chains and release the grip of your past, you are free to grow deeper, to spread wider.

Just as a plant thrives in fresh soil, you, too, will flourish when you surrender to Me. My grace is the soil in which you are planted, and in it, you will grow stronger and more vibrant than you could ever have imagined. Trust in My hand that prunes, that loosens, that prepares. I am always making space for you to grow, for you to bear the fruit I've destined for your life. Let go of what hinders you and trust Me to cultivate in you what I have promised.[29]

---

[29] John 15:1-2

Piece by Piece

As I built LEGO flower bouquet after LEGO flower bouquet, I noticed that each piece — small, seemingly insignificant, and yet crucial — came together to form something so beautiful. The patience it took to follow the instructions, piece by piece, was a reminder of how we, too, are shaped by You, the one who sees the bigger picture even when we can't. We are the LEGO pieces, each of us uniquely crafted and placed by You. And just as the creator of the LEGO set isn't overwhelmed by the pieces that don't fit right or the ones that break, You too are not discouraged by our brokenness. You are not taken aback by our missteps. You are patient, gentle, and unshaken in Your process of building us.

As I moved the pieces from one place to another, things would fall apart or break off. It felt frustrating, especially when I had just put it together and I was certain I knew how to do it. I found myself relying on my own understanding, thinking I could do it again, but it fell apart once more. In my frustration, I had to stop and go back to the instructions. I realized that although I had the right piece in the right place, it was positioned the wrong way. The process was fragile, and, in that fragility, I learned something powerful: the instructions, the guidance, were there all along. It wasn't about my self-reliance or my attempt to control the outcome. It was about trusting the process, following the guidance, and letting go of the frustration when things didn't work out the way I imagined. This process of building is about surrender. You see the full picture. You know the right way, even when I don't. And like the broken pieces I thought I'd failed with, I can trust that You are using everything - the brokenness, the failures, and the triumphs to build something beautiful, piece by piece, in Your perfect timing.

My Way. Not Yours.

Do not try to force an encounter with Me to fit your expectations.

I am not bound by your timelines, your understanding, or your preferences.

I know the deep places of your heart, and I meet you where you are, not where you think I should be.

Stop trying to shape the moment to your liking.

I am the Creator of all things, and I will move in ways that are far beyond what you can imagine.[30]

Trust Me with the encounter.

You do not need to control it, nor do you need to orchestrate it.

Sometimes, you seek Me in ways that you think will bring the closest connection, but I may come to you in the quiet, in the ordinary, or in the moments you least expect. It may not look like you planned, but it will be exactly what you need.

Do not miss My presence because it doesn't meet your expectations.

Let go of your demand for a particular way.

Surrender and allow Me to reveal Myself to you in a way that will deepen your trust, your faith, and your relationship with Me.

I am doing more in the silence, in the stillness, than you realize.[31]

_____

[30] Isaiah 55:8-9

[31] 1 Kings 19:11-12

Trust Beyond Confirmation.

God, there are times when I know what You say, but I still find myself doubting. I just want to be sure. I want more confirmation, Lord. I want to trust You fully, but my heart keeps holding back. It's like I'm wrestling with a part of me that refuses to believe You'll truly come through. I don't want to keep doubting, but the circumstances feel so overwhelming, and I'm afraid I'm not strong enough to believe. You speak clearly, but instead of responding in faith, I find myself asking for more signs, more confirmation, or clearer direction—when, in reality, You have already revealed Your will.

This hesitation often stems from a fear of what obedience will cost or a reluctance to step out of our comfort zone. One of the subtle ways you compromise faith is by delaying obedience under the guise of "waiting for confirmation." While seeking wisdom and discernment is important, your hesitation is rooted in fear and doubt, causing you to disobey Me.
Unbelief is part of your journey. It does not disqualify you from My love. Even those closest to Me wrestled with doubt. It's not about never doubting but about bringing your doubts to Me and allowing Me to transform them into trust. I do not require perfect faith, but a willing heart to surrender. As the father in Mark 9:24[32] prayed, "I believe; help my unbelief." Bring your doubts

---

[32] Mark 9:24

honestly before Me, and I will strengthen you. Your faith doesn't need to be big. Even a mustard seed can move mountains when it is placed in Me.[33] Remember, faith isn't about your ability to believe but about My ability to deliver. Trust in Me, and I will carry you through. While I am merciful and patient, prolonged hesitation can lead to missed opportunities, unnecessary struggles, and even rebellion. You cannot wait for absolute certainty before acting, for faith is about trusting Me, not your ability to hear perfectly. Doubting My ability to guide you often leads to depending on your own reasoning, rather than fully trusting in Me. What does My Word say in 1 Samuel 15:22-23, What is more pleasing to the Lord: your burnt offerings and sacrifices, or your obedience to His voice? Listen! Obedience is better than sacrifice, and submission is better than offering the fat of rams. Rebellion is as sinful as witchcraft, and disobedience is as bad as worshiping idols.[34]

Lord, I repent for disguising my hesitation as discernment. I understand that my delayed obedience is still disobedience My fear of getting it wrong has become a greater focus than my trust in Your ability to lead me. You are not a God of confusion but of clarity, and You do not expect perfection only surrender. If You have spoken, let me not ask You to repeat Yourself out of fear.

---

[33] Matthew 17:20

[34] 1 Samuel 15:22023

If You have called, let me not wait for another sign when faith is my invitation to step forward. I do not want to be so consumed with avoiding mistakes that I fail to move at all. I release the fear of mishearing, mis-stepping, or misunderstanding. I trust that Your voice is louder than my doubt, and if I go astray, You will correct me in love. I will walk in obedience, even if I do it afraid. Even if my steps are shaky, I will move, knowing You uphold me. Lord, help me to respond the first time You speak. Not after overanalyzing, not after seeking validation from others, but at Your word alone. Because You are trustworthy. I surrender the need for certainty and exchange it for faith. I lay down hesitation and pick up trust. I will move because You have spoken.

Plea for Mercy

May Your ears be drawn to our plea for mercy. We come before You, acknowledging the brokenness of our world, our hearts weighed down by doubt, fear, and sin. So many are lost, struggling with unbelief, walking in a false sense of freedom, unaware of the chains that bind us. We ask for Your intervention, for Your Spirit to move mightily among us. Lord, awaken the hearts of Your people. Open the eyes of those who are blind to their need for You and soften the hearts of those hardened by the pressures of this world. Help us, God, to surrender our pride, our self-reliance, and our false hopes.

Draw us closer to You, so that we may know Your truth and find rest in Your presence. I pray for the lost, the weary, the deceived. May we all encounter Your mercy and grace. Pour out Your wisdom and understanding, so that we might live according to Your Word.

May Your peace reign in our hearts, and may we be vessels of Your light to those around us. We thank You. We love You. We honor you and we ask these things of You in the name of Jesus, our Savior and Redeemer.
Amen.

The Turtle's Pace

Just as the turtle moves slowly and steadily, so too is your walk with Me. Know this: the pace I set for you is not a flaw or a delay, but a design.

Just as a turtle carries its shell for protection, I slow your steps to shield you, to help you grow in wisdom, strength, and maturity. You may feel as though you're moving slowly, but trust Me, this is for your protection, for your preparation.

The world may tell you to hurry, to race, to chase after what you desire, but I call you to move with purpose, not in a hurry. Like the turtle, I ask you to take steady, intentional steps, trusting My timing, not your own.

There is no rush when you are walking in My will.

Rest in knowing that I have you covered.

Do not grow weary or discouraged.[35]

Just as the turtle conserves its energy, I ask you to wait on Me, to conserve your strength for the moments when I direct you to move. There is no need to push ahead, for I will show you when the time is right.

---

[35] Galatians 6:9

Know this also: you are uniquely equipped for the journey I've set before you.[36] I am shaping you, teaching you patience, and building endurance in you. I've designed you for this path, for this season, and I will see you through it. I know it feels slow at times, but do not mistake this for a setback.

You are moving exactly as I have ordained.

Trust that every step, even the slow ones, is bringing you closer to the purpose I've placed in your heart.

Your faithfulness in this process matters more than how fast you go.

Keep walking with Me, step by step, and know that I am always with you, guiding you, protecting you, and loving you every step of the way.

---

[36] Hebrews 12:1

Nothing for you. Everything for me. Nothing without me.

Nothing for you.

The desires of the flesh, the world's accolades, and even your own plans, they all pale in comparison to the richness of My love.[37] You were not created to live for the momentary things that pass away. Your purpose, your joy, and your fulfillment are to be found only in Me. You must understand that all you are, all you have, and all you ever hope to be is found in Me. The world around you may tempt you to grasp at things, to hold onto your desires and possessions. But I tell you, these things are temporary. They do not hold the weight of eternity.

Everything for me.

When you surrender everything to Me, your heart, your hopes, your future, you invite My Kingdom to reign fully in your life. Every step, every thought, every action is to be offered to Me in worship, for I am the source of all goodness and life.[38] It is not a loss to give everything to Me — it is a gain.

Nothing without me.

---

[37] 1 John 2:15-17

[38] Romans 12:1

Without Me, you are like a branch severed from the vine, withering and unable to bear fruit. I am the very breath in your lungs, the light in your path. Without My presence in your life, all efforts are in vain. You cannot fulfill your true purpose without Me, for I have made you to long for Me, to walk with Me, and to reflect My glory to the world.

Trust that everything I ask of you is for your good, for your growth, for your peace. I do not withhold from you, but invite you into a deeper relationship with Me. You are not called to a life of striving, but of surrender. You are not called to self-sufficiency, but to utter dependence on Me, the One who created you. In Me, you find your strength, your purpose, your joy. So, release what you cling to and know that in My hands, everything is transformed. You will not lack.[39] In giving everything to Me, you will find all that you truly need.

---

[39] Psalm 34:10

Not Because You Deserve It, But Because I Love You.

Lord, sometimes I feel so unworthy, like I don't deserve to hear from You. I'm afraid that others might see me as unqualified or undeserving, and I begin to question why You would choose me. There are so many others who seem so much more qualified. They have been walking with You for so much longer, their faith seems stronger, their devotion more established. Why me, Lord? Why would You choose someone like me? What if others think I'm somehow different or special because You speak to me? What if they question why You speak to me and not to them? What if they think that I am somehow more deserving than they are? The thought of that brings fear and uncertainty, Lord. I don't want to cause confusion or stir up feelings of jealousy in others.

Do not be afraid. It is not because of your own merit that I speak to you. You haven't earned My love, My attention, or My voice. It is not about your worthiness; it is because of My compassionate heart, My endless love for you, that I choose to be near you, to guide you, to comfort you. I am drawing you close, not because you have done anything to deserve it, but because I desire to be with you.

This will be clear, both to you and to others, that it is not your merit that matters, but My love. It's not about what you've done or what you haven't done; it's about My mercy, My grace, and My longing to be in relationship with you. My heart yearns to reach you, to communicate with you, because I want you to know My love personally. Your worth is not based on your actions or your accomplishments, but on who you are to Me.

You are My child, and I am your Father. You are loved not because of your perfection, but because of My perfection.[40] Let others see My love through you. Let them witness My compassion and grace reflected in your life. It is not because you deserve it, but because I am a compassionate God who reaches out to all. You may feel unworthy, but that is not the truth. Let this truth settle deep within you: I am with you, and I choose you. Your relationship with Me is meant to be a reflection of My desire to touch every heart, not just a few. In this way, you become a living testimony of My grace. You are not meant to be a symbol of your own greatness, but a reflection of My greatness. Let My love flow through you to those around you. It is My love that you carry, not your own worthiness.

I want you to fully receive My love and to understand that it is through My heart, through My desire for you, that you are able to hear My voice. You don't need to feel unworthy or unqualified. My love has already made you worthy. Just as I told Jeremiah: Do not

---

[40] 1 John 3:1

be afraid of them or their hostile faces, For I am with you always to protect you and deliver you.[41] Hear Me, I have put My words in your mouth. I have appointed you for a purpose, to speak My truth, to share My love. Even in your weakness, I am strong.[42] Even when you feel unworthy, I am the One who qualifies you. You are not alone. I am with you always, and I will always be with you to guide you, to comfort you, and to show you the way.

---

[41] Jeremiah 1:8

[42] 2 Corinthians 12:9

A Call to Rise: Unleashing the Fire Within

I am stirring up something powerful within My people. I am raising up a generation of leaders who can no longer contain what I have placed within them. There is a divine urgency rising up, a call to move beyond fear and step boldly into the purpose I've prepared. It's not about rushing ahead prematurely or moving without wisdom, but about being prepared and positioned.

I am raising up leaders who are no longer content with sitting back, bound by hesitation or doubt. These are the ones who feel My fire shut up in their bones, unable to stay silent or stagnant any longer.[43] I am calling them to trade fear for boldness, complacency for courage, and hesitation for decisive faith.

This is a season where intimacy with Me will fuel action, where worship will become the foundation of leadership. As you draw nearer to Me, you are being equipped. Not just with skills but with conviction, not just with knowledge but with the unshakable assurance that I, Myself, am guiding your steps. Now is the time to prepare, to cultivate a spirit that's ready to move when I say move. A spirit no longer held back, but pressing forward with boldness and purpose. The fire within you is not meant to be contained but released, transforming lives and advancing My

---

[43] Jeremiah 20:9

Kingdom. I am calling you to rise up, to let what I have placed within you flow freely—
no longer dormant, but alive, active, and unstoppable.

Shout it aloud, do not hold back. Raise your voice like a trumpet.[44]

---

[44] Isaiah 58:1

"You Are More Than What You Do"

You're quick to run.

Quick to help. Quick to give.

You see needs and respond.

You hear pain and lean in.

You pour out kindness, encouragement, and strength, often without thinking twice.

And I made you this way — full of warmth, overflowing with compassion, eager to carry burdens and lift others up.

Your quickness to love is a reflection of My heart.

Your willingness to serve is beautiful.

But beloved, I never asked you to pour endlessly from a cup you refuse to let Me fill.

I see how tired you've been — how love for others comes easy, but receiving love for yourself feels foreign... even undeserved.

But that's not how I designed you to live.

So now, I'm inviting you to pause.

To stop running.

To stop doing — just for a moment.

And let Me love you in return.

Come sit with Me.

I delight in your servant heart — I always have.

But even more than what you do, I delight in who you are.

You are not just My servant — you are My child.

You are not just a vessel — you are a treasure.

Today, let Me hold you.

Let Me pour healing into the places you've poured from.

You've spent so much time filling others.

Stay still long enough for Me to fill you.

Stay long enough to be held.

Stay long enough to hear My voice speak over you – not as a taskmaster, but as a Father.

Not with demands, but with delight.

You are not just useful.

You are cherished.

Not for how you serve, but simply because you are Mine.

...did you see that?

Lord, from an early age, you know I was taught to grow in independence...

to walk on my own, think for myself, and accomplish things in my own strength. The world praises this kind of self-sufficiency, and somewhere along the way, I started to believe that's what You wanted from me too. I catch myself seeking Your approval through what I've done, like the little sea turtle in Finding Nemo, beaming with pride, saying, "Did You see me?"

But unlike the turtle's dad, You don't seem impressed. And honestly, that confuses me. I want to understand. I want to know why You're not pleased with my effort? Striving and performing feels like all I've ever known to do.

Help me see what You really want from me; beyond the pressure I've placed on myself.

I am not pleased when you seek to live independently of Me—not because I want to withhold from you, but because I know it leads you away from the life I created you for. I did not design you to stand alone but to walk closely with Me. Every good thing you do flows from My grace, not your effort.[45] I don't need your performance; I desire your heart. When you chase self-sufficiency, you step outside the safety and joy of My presence. I want to be

---

[45] Ephesians 2:8-9

the One you run to, the One you depend on—not as a last resort, but as your constant source. Lay down the need to impress Me. I already delight in you, not because of what you do, but because you are Mine. Freedom is found not in standing on your own, but in leaning into Me. Trust Me like a child trusts their Father[46], and let your life reflect deep dependence because it's in that surrender that you will find peace, fulfillment, and the strength you've been trying to earn on your own.

---

[46] Matthew 18:3

Lord, how has pride disguised itself in my life?

Pride deceives you. It convinces you that your worth is something you must earn. That your value is tied to your performance, your image, or your reputation. It tells you that to be loved, you must keep achieving. To be accepted, you must keep striving. But I say to you: You are not what you do. You are not who others say you are. You are Mine.[47]

Pride wears many masks, and in your life, it is often hidden beneath what looks like responsibility, excellence, or even humility. It shows up when you feel the need to prove your worth, when you carry burdens I never asked you to bear, and when you measure your value by what you produce rather than by who I say you are.

Pride convinces you that you must figure things out on your own—that asking for help is weakness, that rest is laziness, and that silence means failure. It causes you to compare yourself to others secretly, either feeling inferior or subtly superior.[48] It fuels the inner critic that shames you for not being "enough," while also resisting correction or surrender.

It's there when you overextend yourself to please people or avoid vulnerability. You call it discipline. I call it fear in disguise.

---

[47] Galatians 6:3

[48] Philippians 2:3-4

But I see through every disguise. I'm not exposing this to shame you. I'm exposing it to free you. Pride cannot remain where My Spirit leads.[49]

I am calling you to a posture that confesses that you need me in every moment and in every detail. Come out from behind the mask. Lay down the exhausting pressure to perform. Let Me strip away everything you've used to protect yourself, because My strength is made perfect in your weakness. Until you fully trust Me to be your source, pride will keep whispering that you must be your own.

---

[49] Proverbs 16:18

Performers Confession

Father, I confess I've been performing. I've been chasing approval from people, from myself, and even from You. I've been measuring my worth by what I do, how well I carry myself, how much I produce, how perfect I appear. It's exhausting and I know it's not what You've called me to.

Somewhere deep down, I've believed the lie that love has to be earned and that if I work hard enough, look good enough, or do enough, I'll finally be enough. Forgive me for the ways I've made performance my identity. Forgive me for the moments I've craved applause more than intimacy with You. I lay down the masks, the striving, the pressure. Help me to believe that being Yours is enough.

From the very beginning, before you did anything, I called you good.[50] Nothing you do can make Me love you more. Nothing you fail to do can make Me love you less. My love is constant and unwavering.[51] But still, you hold try to hold everything tightly in your hands. You try to control outcomes, manage perceptions, and carry burdens I never asked you to. You believe that letting go means losing everything. But you were never meant to be in control. That weight was never yours to carry.

---

[50] Genesis 1:31

[51] Romans 8:38-39

I am the One who holds your life. Nothing is hidden from me.[52] You do not need to prove yourself to Me. I already know you. I know your flaws, your doubts, your fears, and I still choose you. My grace is sufficient for you.[53] You think you must be strong all the time, but I am the strength in your weakness.

You think you must have it all together, but I never asked for perfection. I asked for surrender. So, release the need to perform. Lay down the urge to strive. Stop chasing approval and rest in My acceptance. Let go of the fear that keeps you grasping. Let go of the pride that says, "I must do it on my own." Come to Me. Not when you've fixed everything. Not when you feel worthy.

Come now. Let Me father you, love you, and lead you. Trust Me—not with part of your heart, but with all of it. Even if you fall, I will catch you.

Let Me be enough for you.

---

[52] Hebrews 4:13

[53] 2 Corinthians 12:9

Jesus Striver vs. Jesus Abider?

Father, what's the difference between being a Jesus striver and a Jesus abider? I don't want to get it wrong. Can You explain it to me?

A Jesus striver tries to earn what I've already given. They work hard to prove themselves, thinking their value depends on their performance.[54] Their heart is sincere but striving weighs them down. They live from a place of pressure instead of promise.

A Jesus abider knows they are already loved, already accepted. They stay close to Me, not to earn My favor, but because they know they have it. An abider draws strength from My Spirit, not from their own effort. They bear fruit naturally because they are rooted in Me, not because they are trying harder.[55]

Striving says to self, "I must."
Abiding says to Me, "You will."
Striving exhausts; abiding refreshes.
Striving is about proving; abiding is about trusting.

Rest in Me, and I will accomplish what concerns you.

---

[54] Galatians 5:22-23

[55] John 15:4-5

Abba?

Abba?

They say that means Father...

Safe? Close? But to me... It feels distant.

It feels like something I never really had.

The truth is, I don't know how to be a daughter.

I never learned. The absence, the wounds, the unmet expectations have left spaces in me. Gaps I've tried to fill with performance, perfection, and self-protection.

And now, I find myself doing the same with You.

I call You Father... but I flinch when You come close.

I brace for disappointment. I work for approval.

I wonder if I'm lovable enough to be claimed, to be chosen, to be held.

I've learned how to keep my walls up... but not how to let love in.

But Abba?

Mmhm.

I want to learn.

I want to unlearn the lies that love has to be earned.

I want to lay down the belief that I have to perform to belong.
Teach me what it means to be Your daughter.

Show me the safety of a Father who sees.
The strength of a Father who never grows tired of carrying me.
The consistency of a Father who doesn't change His mind about
me. The mercy of a Father who doesn't hold my failures against
me. The nearness of a Father who leans in when I try to
withdraw. The grace of a Father who knows my flaws but loves
me anyway. The patience of a Father who walks with me at my
pace. The gentleness of a Father who handles my fragile places
with care. The pride of a Father who delights in calling me His own.
The faithfulness of a Father who never walks away — even when
I try to.

Romans 8:15 says I can cry out Abba, Father but I don't know
how to say it without pain. Can I call You Abba with a broken
voice?
Can I bring You this wound and not be turned away?
I'm tired of holding You at a distance.
So here I am...uncertain but reaching for You anyway. Be my
Father.
Not the one I had, but the One I need.

My child, I saw you when your heart first broke
I was there when the silence echoed loud.

I did not abandon you.

I wept with you.

And I have waited, longing for you to come to Me.

I am not the shadow of your father.

I am the fullness of Fatherhood itself.

I am faithful. I protect. I stay.

When you say "Abba,"

it is My Spirit in you crying out,

reminding you:

You are not a stranger here.

You are Mine.

I see every scar.

I know every fear.

And I am concerned with all of it.

I do not dismiss your pain—

I enter it and I redeem it.

You can call Me Abba

with shaking lips and unsure steps.

You can fall into My arms and you will find they have been open all along.

Come closer, beloved.

You are not fatherless anymore.[56]

---

[56] Romans 8:14-17

I love you.[57]

_____

[57] John 3:16

Love You....more.

[Love You More by Anna Golden playing on repeat]

Jesus,

When I look back at all You've done how You found me, carried me, and loved me through every season of my life, I can't help but say:

I love You.

But even more than that, I want to love You more.
Not just with my words. Not just in a song. But with my whole heart. In my choices. In the quiet, hidden places no one sees. In the places I've been scared to let You in.

I want to love You more than my comfort.
More than my fears.
More than my plans... my pride... my control.
I don't want to lose the wonder. Don't let me grow numb to Your presence or take Your mercy for granted.

Teach me what it really means to love You with my life, in surrender, in obedience, in stillness, in trust.

When I feel weak... remind me that even my desire to love You more is a gift from You. It's You working in me.

I don't want to live a single day holding You at a distance.

Let every joy... every trial... every moment... pull me closer.
Break down every wall that keeps me guarded.

You gave everything for me — I want to give You everything in return.

I love You, Jesus.
But I want to love You... more.

Running, But Wanting to Stay

Jesus, sometimes it feels like I don't know how to slow down, like I am incapable. This world... it pulls me. It's fast, loud, always moving. And I hate to admit it, but sometimes... I let it. I get swept up in the rush. The pressure. The need to keep going... to keep doing. But deep down... I don't want to live like this. I don't want to run so fast that I outrun Your presence. I don't want to be so busy planning my future that I miss what You're doing right now. You've never been in a hurry... and yet here I am, racing through life, afraid I'm falling behind when all along, You've been right here, just waiting for me to slow down and notice.

So, Jesus... help me, please Lord.

Search me... slow me... settle me.

Pull me back to stillness.

Quiet the noise inside my head.

I lay my plans... my pace... my pride... at Your feet.

Teach me how to have slow feet the kind that follow.

Teach me to listen before I speak.

To breathe before I rush.

To linger before I leave.

Because the truth is... when I slow down, I see You.

When I'm still, I feel You near.

I don't want to miss Your presence.

[plays slow me down by Charles Weems]

Lingering

God, these days, I find myself lingering.
After church...
After the worship fades...
After the songs have ended and the crowd has moved on... I just stay.

It's not that I don't know how to leave. It's that I'm not ready to.
But because even after the music stops... I can sense that You're still here. Even when the room grows quiet... You stay. And I've realized — I'm starving for these moments. For stillness. For nearness. For You.

The world pulls at me the second I walk out those doors.
The distractions... the noise... the pressure to move on with my day...
And honestly, it feels like everyone is rushing to the next thing.
The conversations. The schedules. The plans.
But in here — in this quiet, after the worship — I feel You.
And I don't want to rush past that anymore.

So I linger.

Not for a show...

Not for a feeling...

But for You...

The One who stays when the music stops.

The One who waits for me to finally slow down.

The One my heart has been longing for... all along.

I'm sorry.

You've been waiting... and I've been distracted.

But I'm here now...

And I want to stay.

Stay as long as you need...I love when you stay.

Why Can't I Stay Full?

You know that lately, I've been wrestling with this quiet but persistent question, Why can't I stay full?

I pour out constantly.
I serve. I give. I encourage. I lead.
I go to the altar. I pray. I fast. I worship. I read the Word.
I do all the things to stay connected, to remain filled...
But still, I end up empty.
Depleted.
Drained.
Like I can't seem to hold onto what I've received.

And here's what's been hardest:
Sometimes I muster up the faith.
I muster up the courage.
I take one step. I write one word, I speak one thing.
But before I even realize it—
that faith, that courage, it feels like it's already gone.
Like I used it up faster than I thought.
Like I poured it out and had no reserve.

But Holy Spirit, You gently showed me the root of it.
There's been a leak.

Not a burst. Not a breakdown. Just a slow, quiet leak.

A place in my soul where the oil has been slipping through.

I didn't notice how much I'd been losing... until I was completely dry.

But in Your mercy, You didn't stop at exposing it.

You began to heal it.

You sealed the unseen cracks.

You patched what was broken.

And You filled me again.

You poured oil.

Over these hands to labor for Your glory.

Over this voice to keep speaking what You give,

Even the hard things.

Even the hidden things.

Even the things I thought I wasn't bold enough to say.

You don't just want me poured out –

You want me whole.

May I be found Faithful

O Lord, hear my cry.

How many times have I said "yes" with my lips but wandered in my heart? You search me and You know me. Nothing is hidden from You.

I cannot pretend before You, though I've tried.

I've tried to cover my lack with effort... with noise... with busy hands.

But I confess, Lord – I've neglected the secret place.

I've chosen comfort over calling.

Convenience over conviction. Busyness over obedience.

I've feared man more than I've feared You.

I've longed to be seen... more than I've longed to be surrendered.

Have mercy on me.

Don't cast me away in my inconsistency.

Teach my feet to follow You even when the path is narrow and unseen.

And yet, in mercy, You still call me Yours.

Have mercy on me, God.

Don't turn away from me in my inconsistency.

Teach my feet to follow You even when the path is narrow... even when it's unseen.

Let my faith not be fleeting, but firm.
Let my yes be rooted in reverence, not emotion.

O God, create in me a clean heart,
And renew a faithful spirit within me.
Break down every idol, every distraction, every wall keeping me
from You.

Lord, I want to be found faithful.

Turn my weakness into worship,
My failures into fuel for deeper devotion.
For You alone are worthy.
You alone are faithful.
Teach me to be like You.

I forgive you.[58]

_____

[58] Ephesians 1:7

What Good is Knowledge Without You?

Lord, my Teacher,
You are the source of all wisdom.
The Giver of knowledge and understanding.
The One who formed my mind.

Thank You for the gift of teaching – for the hunger to study,
to learn, and to rightly divide Your Word.
I want to worship You not just with my lips... not just with my
emotions... but with my thoughts and understanding.

But God, I confess... the temptation is real.
The pull to idolize what I know.
To lean on intellect more than intimacy.
To speak more than I listen.
To teach more than I sit quietly at Your feet.

Keep me low, Lord. Keep me near.
Remind me it's not wrong to worship You with my mind.
You made me this way. You wired me to love truth.
You designed me to hunger for understanding.
But that knowledge was never meant to be hoarded...
Or used to appear superior or to be twisted into self-
righteousness.

Let wisdom never become about platform, applause, or proving a point.
Let it always be about Your glory... and the building up of others in love. You never gave knowledge to be hoarded or used for self-promotion. It was always meant to be poured out in love, in humility, and in worship.

Let knowledge never puff me up,
But always lead me to surrender, to humility, to deeper awe of You.

Teach me to study without striving. To teach without pride.
To be sharp in mind, but soft in spirit.
Help me remain teachable – always aware that no amount of knowledge can compare to knowing You.

Let Your Spirit be the loudest voice. Your Word, the final authority.
Your presence, my deepest pursuit. I yield both my mind and my mouth to You. May they be instruments of worship and truth not tools for self.

I'm not threatened by your questions, your hunger to understand, or your desire to teach.[59] Let your knowledge draw you nearer, not

---

[59] James 1:5-6

higher. Let your wisdom lead you lower, not louder. You don't have to fight to stay low. Stay close... and low will follow.[60]

---

[60] Psalm 25:9

A Complaint Before the Lord

Lord... I don't understand.
We sing about You. We gather in Your name.
We fill buildings and call it church.
But where is the power? Where is the purity?
Where is the hunger that burns for You alone?
We have mastered performance...
But forgotten Presence.
We've traded conviction for comfort.
We follow personalities more than we follow You.
We crave sermons that soothe us, not words that break us.
We chase blessings but avoid surrender.
We post Scriptures... but neglect obedience.
We say we love You... but our lives whisper otherwise.
Lord, we have loved our schedules more than Your Spirit.
We have loved being seen more than being sanctified.
We have loved control... more than we've loved the Cross.

And I'm not exempt.
I've felt the pull the temptation to settle for shallow, safe
religion...
To measure my faith by likes, by applause, by affirmation...
Instead of by love, by holiness, by obedience.
I can't pretend anymore, God.
The cracks are showing. The emptiness is real.

We need You... not just for revival services - but for repentance.
We need You to tear down the idols we've built, even in Your name.
We need You to wake us up... before we drift so far we forget
what it means to belong to You.
Where are You, Lord?
Or maybe...
Where are we?
Have mercy on us.
Call us back.
Interrupt us.
Undo us.
We don't want empty religion.
We don't want performance.
We want You.

Yes, I see it.
You have become lovers of pleasure rather than lovers of Me.[61]
You chase what feels good. What soothes the flesh. What feeds
your pride.
But hear Me. I did not create you for shallow satisfaction.
You covet what your neighbor has. You crave what I never gave.
You demand comfort as if I owe you.[62]

---

[61] 2 Timothy 3:4

[62] Exodus 20:17; James 4:3

Have I not said, you shall have no other gods before Me?[63]
Yet you bow to instant gratification. You serve your cravings.
You call it freedom, but you are not free. You are chained.
You say you love Me but your heart drifts far from Me.
You love My gifts more than you love the Giver.[64]
But still, I am calling you back. Return to Me.

In My presence, not in performance or temporary pleasure, but in
My presence, is fullness of joy.[65] At My right hand are pleasures
forevermore, not the fleeting, empty kind the world offers but
the joy your soul aches for.

Deny yourself. Take up your cross. Follow Me.[66]
This is where life begins. I do not withhold good from you. I
withhold death disguised as desire. I am not holding out on you. I
am protecting you.

Come back to Me.

_____

[63] Exodus 20:3

[64] Isaiah 29:13

[65] Psalm 16:11

[66] Luke 9:23

Love Me with all your heart, your soul, your mind, your strength [67] and I will give you the desires of your heart, not the ones twisted by the world.

You were not made to be ruled by your impulses or shaped by the patterns of this world. I have given you My Word, not to restrict you but to set you free. I have given you My Spirit, not to condemn you but to empower you.
So throw off every weight, every sin that clings so tightly
And run the race I set before you.[68] Fix your eyes on Me. Not on distraction. Not on status. Not on fleeting comforts. Desire Me more than anything else and I will fill you with living water no earthly pleasure can imitate.

I have seen your wandering.
I have watched you chase what sparkles but never satisfies.
I have watched you drink from broken cisterns that hold no water.[69]
But still, My arms are open. Do not mistake My patience for permission or My silence for approval. I am calling you now. Repent, not with empty words, but with your whole heart.[70]

---

[67] Mark 12:30

[68] Hebrews 12:1

[69] Jeremiah 2:13

[70] Joel 2:12-13

Tear down your idols.

Your pride.

Your screens.

Your secret desires.

Your need to be seen.

Come into the light, for I AM light.

Let Me cleanse you. Let Me fill you.

I discipline those I love. This moment is not rejection, it is mercy.[71]

If you humble yourself

If you seek not just My blessings, You will find Me.[72]

I am your portion.

Your joy. Your inheritance. Your reward.

No eye has seen, no ear has heard

What I have prepared for those who love Me.[73]

Choose Me.

Love Me.

I have already chosen you.

---

[71] Hebrews 12:6

[72] Jeremiah 29:13

[73] 1 Corinthians 2:9

So come now, turn from rebellion. Do not harden your heart.[74]

Today is the day of salvation
Now is the hour to return. I stand at the door and knock
If you hear My voice and open the door
I will come in and dine with you, and you with Me. [75]

I have not forgotten you. I will not forsake you.
Though your sins are like scarlet, I will wash you white as snow. [76]

I am the One your soul longs for. Return to Me.
I am merciful. I am gracious. Slow to anger.
Overflowing with steadfast love.[77]

I will restore you.
I will renew you.
And I will rejoice over you with singing.[78]

---

[74] Hebrews 3:15

[75] Revelation 3:20

[76] Isaiah 1:18

[77] Exodus 34:6

[78] Zephaniah 3:17

When Leadership Wounds

Lord... I don't understand it.

I thought they would lead me.

I thought they would guide me, sharpen me, speak life into me.

I thought they were sent to pour into me, to help me grow.

But what I experienced was,

Selfish ambition, masked as wisdom.

Pride, dressed up as confidence and calling.

Control, hidden beneath the language of care and spiritual authority. Manipulation, disguised as prophecy... as You "doing a new thing."

It all sounded right.

It all looked spiritual.

But yet underneath... something was off.

And I could feel it. Yet I stayed, I tried to honor them, honor You. I tried to believe the best, because after all what do I know about any of this? This is why I needed a mentor in the first place!

But quietly, I wrestled...

Confusion knotted my heart.

Disappointment whispered doubts in my ear.

Exhaustion crept in.

Why would You allow me to sit under this person?

To be placed in this space?

What lesson was I missing?

What did I do wrong?

Did I misunderstand Your leading?

Did I mishear Your voice?

And if I'm honest... part of me wondered if You saw. If You cared.

If You would rescue me from it. If I deserved it.

I know it hurt. I saw it all.

I saw how they misrepresented Me.

I saw how it left you confused, exhausted, questioning even My heart. I did not send the pain, but I did not waste it either.[79]

I know it's hard to understand.

I let you see what leadership looks like without humility,

So I could form you into a servant who leads with it.

I let you feel control, so you would choose surrender.

I let you experience manipulation,

So you would cling to truth.

I exposed the striving around you,

To break the striving within you.

The very things that wounded you,

Were the things I was removing from you.

What I endured wasn't wasted... it was refining.

---

[79] Genesis 50:20

It didn't harden me... it humbled me.

It didn't derail my calling... it deepened it.

I see it now... they were never meant to be my source – You always were.

And even through their brokenness, You were still faithful to accomplish Your work in me.[80]

Like oil pressed from olives... something pure was drawn out of the pressure.

I use everything to shape and refine.[81]

The gentle mentors... and the hard ones.

The blessing... and the breaking.

It all has a purpose.

What the enemy meant for harm,

I've used for your becoming.

The crushing produced oil.

The pressure produced purity.

The disappointment produced discernment.

It birthed a heart that longs to serve, not be seen.

A heart that yields, not controls.

A heart that knows... the true call isn't to climb... but to bow.

Thank you Abba... I get it now.

---

[80] Philippians 1:6

[81] Romans 8:28

Let Me be your Shepherd now.

A shepherd does not ask the sheep to map the path,
He simply asks them to follow.
The sheep do not carry their own burdens,
The shepherd carries them.
The sheep do not fight off the wolves,
The shepherd defends them.
The sheep do not strive to find water or pasture,
The shepherd leads them there.[82]

So why do you strive to lead yourself?
Why do you carry what I never asked you to carry?
Why do you fear what I have already gone before you to face?
I have never expected you to be strong enough, wise enough, or
brave enough. I only asked you to stay near to Me.

When you wander, I come for you.
When you fall, I lift you up.
When you are lost, I lead you home.
My rod protects, driving out what seeks to harm you.
My staff corrects, pulling you back when you drift.
My voice guides, steady, familiar, and sure.

_____

[82] Psalm 23:1-3

You were not created to figure it all out.
You were created to follow Me.[83]

So let Me be your Shepherd now,

In your anxious scrolling,

In your packed calendar,

In the late nights where your thoughts won't slow down,

In the mornings where you wake up already overwhelmed,

In the moments you compare your life to theirs,

In the pressure to prove your worth,

In the deadlines,

The group chats,

The endless notifications,

In the silence that feels heavy,

In the noise that feels louder than Me,

In the moments you fake a smile and pretend to be okay,

In the plans you keep trying to control,

In the fears you carry quiet, afraid to name them aloud,

In the moments you feel like you have to do it all, fix it all, carry it all,

Stop.
Breathe.

---

[83] Ezekiel 34:11-12

You were never meant to be your own rescuer.

You were never meant to walk alone.

Let Me be your Shepherd.

Receive My Love by Faith

You keep trying to earn what I have already freely given.

You measure My love by your feelings and your circumstances, but

I do not love like man loves.

My love is constant, and it is not based on how worthy you feel or

on how others treat you. My love is anchored in who I AM,

unshaken, unchanging, and eternal.[84]

You keep waiting to feel worthy,

To see enough evidence,

To prove that you're lovable, but My love was poured out long

before you ever took a breath.

And it does not waver.

This is why I call you to receive My love by faith.

If you wait until you feel worthy,

You'll never rest, for the finish line will keep moving.

If you wait until you have no doubts,

You'll never draw near, for you will always have questions.

If you wait until you've silenced every flaw,

You'll never come at all, for the flaws you fear are the very ones

I came to redeem.

_____

[84] Isaiah 54:10

If you wait until your life is spotless,

You will miss the invitation to grace altogether.

If you wait until the scars are gone,

You'll never know the Healer who calls you beloved, scars and all. If you wait until you've earned your way in,

You will stand outside forever — for no one earns that for which I've already paid.

I never told you to fix yourself.

I never asked you to prove your worth.

I told you to come.[85]

Just as you are.

Worn.

Weary.

Wounded.

Unsure.

Messy.

Afraid.

I told you to come.

To believe.

To receive.

My love has never been dependent on your ability to get everything right.

_____

[85] Hebrews 4:16

It has always been dependent on who I AM —[86]

Faithful.[87]

Unchanging.[88]

Merciful.[89]

Sure.

So lay down the measuring stick.

Lay down the impossible checklist.

Lay down the shame that keeps you distant.

And by faith...

Simply receive Me.

_____

[86] Exodus 34:6-7

[87] Psalm 100:5

[88] Hebrews 13:8

[89] Psalm 136:1

I believe, Help my Unbelief?

Father,

I've been sitting with Mark 9:24[90] : "I believe... help my unbelief."

How can both be true at the same time?

How can someone *believe* and still need help with unbelief?

Is that me?

Do I have unbelief?

Because... I believe in You.

I believe in Your Word.

I teach it.

I quote it.

I pray it.

I've built my life on it.

But... is there still unbelief in me?

Are You showing me cracks I've ignored?

Have I mistaken confidence in knowledge

For actual trust in You?

Have I trusted You with my words

But not always with my steps?

My mind says "Yes, Lord"...

But my hesitation... my control... my constant need for a backup plan...

What do *they* say?

_____

[90] Mark 9:24

My child... you're beginning to see it.

Belief is not the absence of struggle; it's the presence of
surrender. You believe... but there are corners of your heart still
clinging to control. You speak My truth, and I love that... but
sometimes you brace for disappointment while you pray.

You obey... but only when it feels safe.

You trust Me... but you still check for escape routes.

That's not failure, it's humanity.

And that's exactly why I meet you there.

I never asked for perfect belief... only honest surrender.

Bring Me your gaps... your fears... your "almost" obedience.

I'll fill the cracks with grace.

I'll help your unbelief... not with shame, but with love.

So, yes... you believe.

And yes... you still need My help.

But that's the invitation,

not the disqualification.

Come closer.

I'll teach you to trust.

Tick, Tick, Tick..

Lord, You showed me something today,

A picture I can't unsee.

The enemy... at a gas stove.

Moving from knob to knob.

Fingers steady, eyes patient.

Testing. Turning.

Tick, tick, tick...

Trying each one, turning it slowly,

Tick, tick, tick...

waiting for one to ignite.

Turning each knob, deliberately.

Anger, insecurity, pride, shame, performance,

He knows them well... my fault lines.

He remembers what once ruled me.

He tracks my patterns,

Keeps record of my weaknesses,

Waiting for just the right mixture

Of pressure...

Of weariness...

Of opportunity...

To twist the right knob

And spark destruction.

And when one flame doesn't catch,

he doesn't flinch,

Tick... tick... tick...

Persistent.

Tick... tick... tick...

Strategic.

Tick... tick... tick...

Subtle.

But You, Lord...

You are teaching me the unseen war behind the stove.

You are uncovering the slow leaks.

The subtle places in my soul where sin breathes beneath the

surface. Where I've grown careless, where I've mistaken the

absence of flame

For safety.

But there's danger in the gas that lingers,

In the small allowances I excuse,

In the quiet whispers of "It's not that bad..."

But it is.

So You're teaching me to keep the gas off.

To turn the valves tight with repentance.

To seal the cracks with surrender.

To stop flirting with the hiss of temptation

Just because no fire has caught... yet.

You're training my hands for war—

Not with matches, but with discipline.

Not with arrogance, but with watchfulness.

You're tuning my ears to the ticking

Not as background noise,

But as warning.

As mercy. As Your voice, calling me higher.

A call to holiness. A call to vigilance.

A call to courage. A call to keep my heart—

Fully fixed...

Fully surrendered...

Fully Yours.

So next time I hear... tick... tick... tick...

I won't dismiss it.

I won't linger near the stove, curious.

I'll recognize the setup,

The subtle twist of the knob,

The quiet hiss of compromise.

And I'll run—

Not in fear, but in wisdom.

Back to You. Back to safety.

Back to the place where the flame never destroys— Only refines.

Death Dressed as Devotion

I was devoted once.

Not to Christ.

But to the chains that nearly killed me.

I was devoted once... to alcohol.

It had my time.

It had my trust.

It had my body.

It had my worship.

I arranged my life around the next pour,

bowed my body to the buzz,

numbed the ache and called it coping...

But it was worship.

Worship at the feet of my own destruction.

I was devoted once... to relationships.

I gave them my heart.

I gave them my soul.

I gave my identity piece by piece,

to people who couldn't save me.

I sacrificed myself on the altar of attention.

I laid my worth down at the feet of rejection.

I let lust become my priestess, guiding me to the altar of false comfort, where I traded truth for temporary relief.

And I called it love.

But it was idolatry... dressed up as intimacy.

I was devoted once... to the altars of my ancestors.

I called on the names of the dead.

I burned incense to demons wrapped in tradition.

I set the table for spirits that only came to steal.

I opened the door.

I let them sit. I let them speak.

I let them torment me and I still called it "spiritual"...

as if that made it holy.

But it was slavery. It was deception.

It was death... dressed as devotion.

I was devoted once...

Fully.

Blindly.

Recklessly.

To everything that kept me bound.

So now...

How could my devotion to Christ be less?

How could I give Him half,

when I once gave darkness everything?

How dare I worship casually now,

when the blood of Jesus shattered the grip of torment,

evicted every intruder in my soul,

and broke the altars I once bowed at?

He silenced the voices that used to scream through my mind.

He walked straight into the middle of my bondage

and paid for my release... in full.

So this is my devotion now:

Not quiet.

Not cautious.

Not polite.

It is loud.

It is relentless.

It is fire on the altar... every single day.

Because I know what it cost Him.

And I remember what He pulled me from.

So I worship...

With my body – because I once used it to betray Him.

With my life – because I once gave it to everything but Him.

With my yes – poured out like oil, without conditions, without

excuses –

because I once poured myself out for idols that only emptied me

in return.

But now... I belong to Jesus.

My devotion is my response to freedom.

My worship is war.

My surrender is fire.

My life is proof.

And I will not – I cannot – forget the pit He pulled me from.

Buried Rivers, Silent Wells

I didn't place treasure inside you for it to stay buried.
What I deposited in you was never meant to be hidden, hoarded,
or held back.[91]

I gave you those gifts, not just to bless you but to flow through
you.
You were not designed to be a reservoir.
You were created to be a river.
Let it move. Let it pour out.

Why are you burying what I've entrusted to you?
Fear? Insecurity? Comparison?
Do you really believe I didn't know what I was doing when I chose
you?

I never asked you to be perfect, just faithful.
What you carry was shaped in My presence. Formed through fire.
Cultivated in secret.
And now you're trying to keep it safe?

Don't protect what I told you to pour.

---

[91] Matthew 25:14-30

Don't bury what I called you to multiply. [92]

I didn't give you the word for it to stay in your journal.
I didn't give you the testimony for it to stay untold.
I didn't give you the revelation for it to die in your notebook.
I didn't give you the fire for it to stay contained.
I gave it to you to release.

Stop waiting for permission when I've already given you a commission.
Stop shrinking back. Stop second-guessing.
I'm not asking for your perfection, I'm asking for your yes.

And don't worry about the results.
Obedience is your responsibility. Impact is Mine.

I'm not looking for collectors, I'm looking for carriers.
I'm not impressed with how much you store,
but how willing you are to pour until you're empty. [93]

You say you want to hear, "Well done."
Then don't die full.
Don't leave the earth with your gift still inside you.

---

[92] 1 Peter 4:10

[93] John 7:38

Don't spend your life preserving what was meant to be poured out like oil.

The world doesn't need a more polished version of you.
It needs the anointed one I've called, equipped, and set apart.

Now pour it out.

Walls of Jericho

There are some walls in your life that won't fall by force.
Not by striving. Not by strategy.
But by obedience.
By worship.
By faith.

That's what I taught Joshua.

The walls of Jericho weren't shaken by human strength,
they were shattered by surrendered steps.
I told My people to march when it looked ridiculous.
To circle when it made no sense.
To shout when they saw no cracks.
And they obeyed Me before they saw the breakthrough.[94]

This is what I'm asking of you, too.

I know you've been praying for things to break.
I see you walking around situations that feel impossible.
Barriers that look too thick. Cycles that seem too long.
But I need you to trust Me like Joshua did.

Not just with your heart, but with your feet.

---

[94] Joshua 6:1-20

Because some walls only fall when your faith starts moving.
Some chains only break when your voice rises in praise.
And some victories are reserved for those who obey when it feels foolish.

Jericho wasn't just about walls falling, it was about hearts trusting.
It was about a people who dared to believe that My way is better, even when it doesn't make sense.
That My timing is perfect, even when it feels slow.
That My instructions carry power, even when they sound strange.

So here's what I want you to know:

You don't have to fight to break the wall,
You just have to walk with Me until I say, "Shout."

You don't have to force the outcome,
You just have to follow the last thing I said.

You don't need to see cracks,
You just need to believe that I am faithful.

Let go of your need to understand and grab hold of your call to obey.

This next breakthrough won't come by might or by power,
but by My Spirit.

And when the walls fall, it won't be because of what you did.
It'll be because of Who you walked with.

So march again.
Circle again.
Praise again.
Don't grow weary in the walking.
Don't lose your shout in the silence.
Your obedience is shaking the unseen.

And when I say, "Now,"
the walls will fall.

Full But Never Fed

God, why is it that when my soul is starving,
I run to the fridge instead of Your feet?
I tell myself I'm hungry but I'm not. Not really.
It's not my stomach that's empty.
It's the places in me that feel overlooked, unseen, anxious, bored,
lonely, tired, ashamed. I stand in the kitchen looking for
something to fill me.
I call it a snack.
You call it what it is –
a quiet cry for something deeper.

Somewhere along the way, food became my therapist.
My comforter. My escape from the moments when life feels too
loud,
When I feel too much, or when I don't want to feel anything at
all.

The crunch numbs the chaos. The sweet silences the sorrow.
But only for a moment.
And then the shame rolls in.
full-body, empty heart.

Lord... this isn't about food.
It's about misplaced hunger.

It's about trying to satisfy a craving only You can touch.
It's not calories I'm desperate for, it's communion.
It's not sugar I'm chasing, it's You.

But I keep feeding my flesh,
While You stand there table set,
Offering the only thing that satisfies.

I've bowed my head more quickly over fast food meals and
desserts than I've run to Your presence. Forgive me.

Break the chains Lord,
Not just the midnight snacking or the secret cravings,
But the lie underneath it all.
The lie that says food can fix what only You can fill.
Help me trade the high of indulgence
For the healing of intimacy with You.

Let me taste and see that You are good.
Better than ice cream.
Better than cookies, cakes, and carbs.
Better than the temporary things I keep trying to patch this
God-sized ache with.
Fill me, Lord. Not with food, but with You.
My hands betray me,
Forks and fingers digging into what never truly satisfies.

Tear down the altar I've built.

Uproot the idol I've made of my cravings.

Teach my body to feast on Your Word again.

Teach me to hunger and thirst for righteousness.[95]

I don't want to be stuffed... and still starving.

I want to be filled...really filled,

By every word that comes from Your mouth.

So here I am, Lord.

Not hiding behind snacks,

Not bowing my head over drive-thru bags,

But bowing my heart before You,

The only One who satisfies.

---

[95] Matthew 5:6

Tomorrow

Lord,

I don't know when rest turned into resistance.

When "just five more minutes" became five more days.

When I stopped stewarding what You gave me

and started letting it all collect dust.

I say I'm tired, but the truth is, I'm avoiding.

Avoiding the weight of purpose.

Avoiding the stretch of discipline.

Avoiding the mirror that responsibility holds up to my soul.

I call it a break.

You call it bondage.

Every unchecked item on my to-do list,

every task I've postponed,

every gift I've shelved,

it all becomes bricks in the wall between You and me.

You've given me vision,

and I've buried it beneath convenience.

You've whispered "move,"

and I've hit the snooze button on You.

Forgive me Lord.

I scroll instead of seek. I nap instead of knock.

I binge shows when I should be breaking cycles.

My flesh wants easy. My spirit is dying for purpose.

Lord, I repent, not just for my inactivity,

but for believing that procrastination is harmless.

It's not. It's choking out the fruit I was meant to grow.

It's muffling Your voice with blankets of delay.

You didn't save me so I could stay stuck.

You didn't call me just to watch me coast.

Wake me up.

Stretch me out.

Shake the dust off my gifts and put a fire in my bones.

Replace my laziness with a holy drive.

Replace my excuses with obedience.

And when I feel overwhelmed, remind me that You don't need me

to do it perfectly, You just need me to move when You say "go."

I'm done letting the enemy rock me to sleep

when You're trying to raise me up.

I'm ready now.

Not tomorrow.

Now.

...Takes one to know one.

Lord,

I've been hurt by one sided friendships.

I know what it feels like to only be called when someone needs

something.

To be the "safe space" for others,

but never invited in when the joy hits.

To be the listening ear, the late-night lifeline,

the ride, the place to crash, the go-to for advice

but not the one chosen just to be with.

I've cried over it.

Felt used. Invisible. Taken for granted.

It's lonely to be needed but not known.

Guess it takes one to know one, huh?

Because now I see,

I've done the same to You.

This has been a one-sided friendship.

One where I've done all the needing,

and You've done all the giving.

I've treated You like an Uber,

summoning You when I need a quick way out.
Like an Airbnb,
expecting comfort and peace,
but only staying long enough to rest and go.
Like a therapist,
dumping the weight of my problems,
then disappearing before You could speak healing.

You've always been a Friend,
faithful, present, personal.
But I've been transactional.
I've known You as Helper, Healer, Rescuer
but I haven't been a good friend to You.
And for that... I'm sorry.

You're the only one who's stayed.
The only one who listens without growing weary.
The only one who's never used my pain as ammunition,
never tired of my voice,
never left me on read.
And still, I've come to You with hands out
and not enough gratitude.

I've pulled on Your power,
but neglected Your presence.
I've wanted breakthrough,

but not friendship.

And now that I feel it,
the ache of being needed but not seen,
of being called on but not cared for,
I can only imagine how deeply it must grieve You.
It hurts my heart when it's done to me,
so, I know it breaks Yours.

Forgive me, Friend.
Forgive my distance.
Forgive the way I've prioritized everything and everyone over You.
How I've cried, wanting someone to just see me and sit with me,
while You've been waiting-quietly,
faithfully-on the couch the whole time.

Teach me to sit with You, not because I need something,
but because I need You.

Let our friendship be real, woven into the quiet,
the laughter, the ordinary, the everything.

I don't want to just know what You can do.
I want to know You.

I know. [96]

---

[96] Psalm 139:1-4

Only in theory

You say you trust Me but only in theory.
You sing "I surrender all," but only in theory.
You quote My Word, believe it, even,
but still hold back the parts of your life that scare you most.

You worship when it's safe.
You declare My faithfulness while secretly building backup plans in
case I don't come through.
You say I'm your Provider, but panic when the account dips.
You say I'm your Healer but let fear speak louder than My name.
You say I'm your Shepherd but only follow Me when the path
makes sense.
You say I'm your Peace but still cradle your anxiety like it's your
responsibility to carry.

Belief in theory isn't enough for where I'm taking you.
I'm calling you into practice.[97] Into lived faith. Into obedience
when it costs. Into worship when you don't feel like singing.
Into prayer that isn't cute and curated, but messy and real.
Into trust that holds on even when your timeline shatters.

Do you love Me enough to live what you say you believe?
To give when it's inconvenient?

---

[97] James 2:17

To wait when it's uncomfortable?

To say yes when you don't yet understand? [98]

This isn't about performance. This is about formation.

I'm shaping your life into a living testimony—not just a memorized one.

I'm not after your perfection—I'm after your participation.

Will you practice faith when the feelings fade?

Will you trust Me with your future while it's still unclear?

Will you follow Me when it means laying down your own plans?

I'm not calling you to pretend.

I'm calling you to practice.

Come closer.

Let Me teach you what it means to believe—with your life, not just your lips. [99]

---

[98] Mark 8:34, Luke 9:23, Matthew 16:24

[99] James 1:22

Necessary Work

I have not forgotten you.[100]
What I am cultivating in you right now is not wasted time, it is necessary. You keep asking Me what's next, but if I showed you the full picture before the roots of trust were deep, you'd try to run ahead of Me. This season is not punishment. It's preparation.

The silence you feel is not distance. It's an invitation.
Closer. Still. Closer.

I'm pulling you into a trust that lives beyond theory.
This is the kind that steadies your hands when you can't see the outcome.
The kind that keeps your heart anchored when the doors stay shut.
The kind that teaches you to rely on Me, not just with words—but with every step.

You may feel like nothing is moving, but I assure you that everything is being made ready. You can't yet see the weight of the work I've prepared for you, but I am shaping your character to match your calling.

---

[100] Isaiah 49:15-16

Let Me finish what I started.[101]

Let Me deepen your faith until it's not just belief, but muscle.

Let Me teach you how to be still without giving up.

Because where I'm taking you, you'll need to know how to trust Me even in the dark.

Stay near,

I'm working[102],

on it and on you.

_____

[101] Philippians 1:6

[102] Jeremiah 18:6

Poured Out

I will pour it out every gift, every word, every assignment.
I will leave nothing buried,
withholding nothing that He has entrusted to me.

I choose obedience over outcome, trusting that my yes is enough.
I know I was given to give, not to hoard, hide, or hesitate.

I want to be poured out like oil at His feet.[103]
I recognize that this oil is for pouring, not preserving.
I will be faithful with the flame, fanning it rather than fearing
it.

No more holding back. Not my time, not my gifts, not my voice.
Every gift, on the altar.

That is my offering.
That is my worship.

---

[103] John 12:3

Search Me

Lord,

Search me. Strip me.

Expose the hidden places I've dressed up as "calling."

You called me to lead,

But have I made it about being seen more than about serving?

Have I craved the influence... more than intimacy with You?

Have I sought platforms over prayer?

Applause over obedience? Position over presence?

I must ask myself,

Am I leading because You've called me to pour out what You've placed in me...

Or because I crave the honor that comes with being called "Leader"?

Am I teaching because I long to equip and disciple,

or because I like the sound of my voice echoing in rooms full of affirmation?

Purge me, God.

I don't want to say Your name but build my brand.

I don't want to quote Your Word while secretly living for recognition.

I don't want to preach light while walking in hidden pride.

Purify my motives until my "yes" is for Your glory alone.
Until when I speak, it sounds like You.
Until when I serve, it smells like humility.
Until when I lead, it looks like You Jesus.

If it keeps me from the secret place, if it's feeding my ego.
If it's muting Your voice in me, take it.

Let me be known in heaven before I ever seek to be known on earth.
Let my leadership flow from love.
Let my influence be drenched in Your Spirit, not my striving.
And let everything I do preach one message: All glory to You, God.

You hear me.

Lord, I'm learning to trust that I hear You.
That You speak.
That I'm not just talking into the wind and calling it prayer.
You've been patient with my doubts, kind with my questions, and faithful to show me that You really do lead me—gently, but clearly.

But now...
You're stretching me in a new way.
It's not just about me hearing You anymore.
It's about trusting that You hear me.

That when I whisper prayers too quiet for others to notice, You lean in.
That when I bring the same request again, and again, and again...
You don't tune me out.
That I'm not just another noise in a world full of voices.
That my heart, my thoughts, my trembling faith matter to You.

It's one thing to say I believe You speak.
It's another to believe You listen.
And I feel You are inviting me to rest in that truth:
You hear me.

Not because I prayed the perfect way.

Not because I proved I was worthy.

But because I'm Yours.

So here I am.

Just honest and that's enough.

Fisher of men or fisher of demons?

There is a hunger in the earth for revelation.
For understanding. For power.
But not all hunger is holy and not every insight leads to freedom.

There's a way the world, even My people can become fascinated with naming darkness. Every struggle becomes a spirit. Every trial becomes a curse.
Every emotion becomes a sign of some hidden force at work.

Yes, the battle is real. Yes, the enemy prowls.
But child don't lose sight of Me trying to study him.[104]

Did I ask My disciples to be fishers of men, or fishers of demons?[105]
I gave you power over the enemy, not so you would obsess over him, but so you would walk in victory and lead others into freedom.
Your authority is not for spotlighting the works of darkness, it's for destroying them and lifting up the name that saves.

You are not called to chase down every shadow, but to carry My light.

---

[104] James 4:7

[105] Matthew 4:19 , Mark 1:17

Your armor was not given so you could become a spiritual detective.

So when you're tempted to chase "what spirit is this?"

Return to Who I Am.

The Cross already exposed, disarmed, and defeated every principality.[106]

Fix your eyes back on Me.

Keep your gaze clear.

And remember—

Revelation without love, without truth, without Me... is just noise.

---

[106] Colossians 2:15

A Monument of Mercy

Today I shared my testimony with someone who says they follow
You. I did it out of obedience,
out of love for You,
to point back to Your power and mercy.
But Lord... it didn't feel like they saw You in it.

I felt like I was on display.
Like an exhibit in a museum of bondage.
It's like they were analyzing the pit You pulled me from more
than Your hand that pulled me out.
It was as if the miracle became secondary to the mess,
as if my chains and deception became more interesting than Your
glory.

That grieved my heart Abba. It made me sad.
Not because I'm ashamed of what You've delivered me from,
but because they missed You and I wanted them to see You.

Help me not to retreat into silence,
But also not to confuse applause or curiosity with true
transformation.
Help me to rest in the truth that even when people are
distracted by the before, You are still writing the after.

And even if only You see the fullness of what You've done... that's enough.

I lay this ache at Your feet.
I trust You to use my story even when it's misunderstood.
Even when it's mishandled.
Even when it becomes spectacle instead of testimony.

You were glorified in my obedience and that's what matters most

I saw your love for Me in every word you shared.
I know it hurts when your story is treated like spectacle instead of sacred. But remember the fragrance of your testimony is not wasted.[107]

It rises before Me as worship.
I don't measure fruit by their reaction.
Do not retreat.
Do not let misunderstanding silence you.
You are not a museum of mistakes.
You are a monument of mercy.

_____

[107] Revelation 12:11

I am the Author of your after.[108]
And even if they miss it,
I never miss it.
You glorified Me today.
And that is never in vain.

---

[108] Hebrews 12:2

The Weight I Can't Name

Why am I discouraged?
Why is my heart so sad?
I will put my hope in You God!
I will praise You again,
my Savior and my God![109]

Some days, Lord, the heaviness just comes.
I don't know why. Nothing specific happened.
But still, I feel off. Unsettled. Irritable. Low.
Like something is sitting on my chest, but I can't name it.
I just know it's there. And I know You see it.

Thank You for not asking me to pretend.
Thank You that I don't have to explain myself to be understood
by You. You know my thoughts before I speak them, and You feel
the ache in my soul even when I can't put it into words.
I bring this weight to You not so You can fix my feelings, but
because I trust You to hold me through them.

Help me not to retreat into numbness or frustration. Help me
not to shame myself for being in this place.
Instead, teach me to lean into You right here—honestly and fully.

---

[109] Psalm 42:11

I choose to put my hope in You.
Even when I don't feel it yet.
Even when the fog hasn't lifted.
Even when praise feels more like a whisper than a shout.
Still—I will praise You.

Not because I understand what's going on inside me,
but because I know who You are.
Let Your peace settle the unrest in my spirit.
Let Your joy begin to rise and anchor me again.
Remind me where my hope comes from, it comes from You.

I trust that You are near, even now.
You haven't left.
You're not disappointed in me.
You're present and that's enough.
So I'll wait with You in this place, confident that joy will come,
but content to worship You even before it does.

The enemy lied to me today...

The enemy lied to me today,
and my feelings agreed with him.
El Roi, I need to tell You what he said.

He told me I'm alone.
That no one's really in my corner.
He said I'm always the strong one
because no one else knows how to be.
...and my feelings agreed with him.

He told me if I don't do it, it won't get done.
That I'm the one holding everything together.
That I have to show up even when I'm empty
because no one notices when I'm running low.
...and my feelings agreed with him.

He told me I'm easy to forget.
That when people don't reach out,
it's because I'm not worth remembering.
He said I pour more than I ever receive.
...and my feelings agreed with him.

He said I'm too much.
He said I'm not enough.

He said I'm both at the same time.
And somehow... my feelings agreed with him.

He twisted silence into rejection.
He turned tired eyes into proof of abandonment.
He used the ache in my heart
as evidence that I must not be loved.
And for a moment... my feelings agreed with him.

But You, Abba...
I know Your voice.[110]
And this wasn't it.

So I'm telling on him.
Because I'm Yours.
And I know You don't let lies slide.

You remind me that I'm never alone.
That You go before me, stand beside me, dwell within me.
You lift burdens I didn't even know I was carrying.
You hold me when I'm too tired to hold myself.

You defend me, protect me, love me fiercely.

---

[110] John 10:27

So I'm here, in your presence asking that You let truth wash over the places where lies tried to live.
Because when I'm with You,
even my feelings remember what's real.

Psalm 23[III]

Just like sheep, we are prone to wander. That is why, just like sheep, we are in desperate need of a Shepherd. Lord, You are our Shepherd. That means You feed us, tend to us, heal us, guide us, defend us, protect us, and watch over us. The truth is, we don't always know what we need or what's best for us. That's why You are our Shepherd. You know when we need green pastures, and You know when still waters are best. You want us to depend on You for everything. No matter what it looks like around us or how we feel, we are covered. We are not lacking anything that You cannot provide. You are the Creator of all things, and You know exactly how to tend to all things, including us.

You know we've been hurt. And You want to comfort us—not just in select moments, but always. We've been conditioned to believe we must protect ourselves. That we must be strong enough, wise enough, independent enough. But You never asked us to fight alone. You are our Protector. You are our Comfort. The days of us fighting alone are over. Your rod and Your staff—they are not symbols of aggression, but protection. They set boundaries. They ward off threats before they can ever get close. You want us to know that even in the valley, especially in the valley, You are right here. And we will make it through. Not alone, but with You.

[III] Psalm 23

Help us stop counting ourselves out of Your anointing. Help us stop believing the lie that we are too broken, too behind, too inconsistent, too afraid. You're not looking for perfection; You're calling us to surrender. To trust. To walk closely.

Be open to correction. With Me, you have all you need. If I've yet to provide it, you've yet to need it. Stop worshiping productivity. I want to give you rest.

You want to free us from the very things that keep us far from You. You will love us to the point where the pain of our past loses its grip. You know we're scared.

You have no reason to be. I am right here.
The valley is dark, but the shadow of death is only that—a shadow. Shadows require light. And that light is proof that You are with us. The danger is perceived, not real. No evil will conquer us because we are in Your protection wherever we go.

We can sit in confidence, even in the presence of our enemies, because Your protection cannot be defeated. You prepare a table for us in front of them. You anoint our heads with oil *while they watch*. Our cups overflow with blessings. Our enemies don't intimidate You. They shouldn't intimidate us either. And when the darkness starts to close in, let the shadow remind us that there has to be light for there to be a shadow.

Your light Is still with us. Let
Your love and Word light our way.

We are not victims. Your Spirit lives within us. Fear no longer has a
hold. We no longer have to turn to the things we once did for
comfort or survival. You are our rest. You are our victory. You will
restore everything the enemy tried to steal. Your goodness and
mercy will follow us—not just on good days, but every day. The
valley won't be with us always. But Your presence will be.
You are asking us to surrender. To repent. To let You restore our
souls and renew our strength. You're not disappointed in us. You
want to replenish us. You want to lead us down the right path—not
to control us, but to bring honor to Your name through our lives.

When David said, "The Lord is my Shepherd," [112] he was claiming
ownership. Submitting. And as he wrote, something shifted. He
started talking about You, but then began talking to You.

That's what happens in the valley. It draws us closer. It reminds
us that You're not far. That You're not just going before us like
You did with Israel, You're right beside us. David didn't say, He is
with me." He said, YOU are with me. The tense changed. The
relationship deepened.

_____

[112] Psalm 23:1

It became repentance. A realization. A re-centering.
We were trying to figure it out ourselves, but YOU—You restore us.

You lead us. You comfort us. You've never left.
And then came the assurance: "Surely, Your goodness and unfailing love will pursue us all the days of our lives."[113]

We may have wandered, but You pursued. We may have feared, but You protected. We may have doubted, but You remained.
We cannot outrun Your goodness. We cannot cancel Your mercy.
We cannot disqualify ourselves from Your love.

We will dwell in the house of the Lord forever[114]—on this earth, and thereafter. That means we will live in Your presence. Not as visitors. As Your sheep.

You want us to understand the power of Your presence. If You are beside us, we cannot be touched. The enemy may come close, but he cannot conquer. The shadow may fall, but it cannot harm. Your light creates the shadow.

The shadow is the evidence of Your nearness.

---

[113] Psalm 23:6

[114] Psalm 23:6

We may have forgotten You were there—but You never left.
You are right beside us. We are Yours. You are ours.
And surely—yes, surely—Your goodness and mercy are still chasing us.[115]

Today. Tomorrow. And forever.

_____

[115] Psalm 23:6

Expect an outpouring

My people, must learn to be content with the partial picture until I choose to reveal more.

You do not need to know what to do. It does not all have to make sense. You do not need all the answers.

For My thoughts are not your thoughts, neither are your ways My ways.[16]

Here is what you must know:

How to hear My voice.

How to trust My Word.

How to depend fully on Me for all things.

How to stay near Me, to remain in My presence, and to seek My face with your whole heart.

Bring Me your questions, especially when you do not understand what I am saying or showing you.

If you do this, if you will remain close, then even without full understanding, you will experience what I have promised:

Expect an outpouring.

---

[16] Isaiah 55:8

Did I not speak to Daniel? When he did not understand, I told him: "Go your way, Daniel, for the words are sealed until the time of the end. Many shall be purified, made spotless and refined... but the wicked will continue to be wicked. None of the wicked will understand, but those who are wise will understand."[117]

Children, there is much to come things that will be difficult to grasp.

But I will give wisdom to the righteous in My perfect timing.

There is a time of suffering ahead.

A time more severe than anything you have seen.

In those days, your idols will not be able to save, sustain, comfort, or provide for you.

I am calling for a remnant, disciples who will not be shaken by what is coming.

There will be war.

There will be famine.

There will be persecution.

There will be death.

But I will rescue My people.

Do not fear. I am just, and I am faithful. I will do all that I have spoken.

---

[117] Daniel 12:8-10

These days will break the pride, arrogance, and self-sufficiency of a rebellious people.

Did I not say in Amos 4

"I brought hunger to every city and famine to every town. But still you would not return to Me... People staggered from town to town for water but did not get enough to drink. Yet you have not returned to Me." [118]

Turn to Me, and you will find safety.

Even in the darkest days, those who return to Me will be delivered from the grip of sin and death forever.

But far too many of My people are consumed with the cares of today and the worries of tomorrow.

You've taken your eyes off Me.

You try to fix your life without fixing your gaze.

But like Jehoshaphat said: "We do not know what to do, but our eyes are on You." [119]   They expected an outpouring and so must you.

Many sing My name, speak of Me, and even serve in My name, but their hearts are far from Me. There is no real repentance. No real desire to please Me.

Their lips honor Me, but their hearts are loyal to idols.

---

[118] Amos 4:6-8

[119] 2 Chronicles 20:12

But I say to you now: The idols are falling.

The high places will be torn down.

Jobs, titles, talents, wealth, relationships, influence, reputation—none of it will save you.

Only I can.

This is your invitation:

Return to Me.

Repent.

Expect the outpouring.

I need My people awake.

Open your ears, your eyes, your hearts, your minds,

not just in the natural, but in the Spirit.

Expect an outpouring.

Do not be deceived by appearances.

Remember, I, the Lord your God, came into the world in a form many did not expect.

Their expectations caused them to miss Me. Do not miss Me now.

I have a way of revealing Myself to those who are truly seeking.

Stay close. Prioritize intimacy with Me.

Make time for silence, stillness, fasting, prayer, worship.

You cannot clearly hear My voice if you've already decided what you want Me to say.

Take the posture of Job when I answered him out of the whirlwind:

"I am nothing—how could I ever find the answers? I will cover my mouth with my hand. I have said too much already. I have nothing more to say."[120]

Just listen.
Just trust.
And expect the outpouring.

Don't waste your energy trying to figure out mysteries I have not revealed.
Stop focusing on what lies ahead, and focus on Who is ahead.
I AM.
Rest in the truth that I am sovereign.
Hope in the name of Jesus, your Savior and King.
Church, ready yourselves.
Be postured for My return.

Do you recognize the sound of the trumpet?
Can you feel the wind of My Spirit rushing near?
What a tragedy it would be...
To miss the outpouring of My Spirit.

Do not miss it.

_____

[120] Job 40:4-5

Cry out to Me:

"Lord, don't let me miss it."

"Lord, help me discern."

"Lord, keep me from becoming one of the proud, the unfaithful, or the self-centered."

I, the Almighty, desire to pour out My presence upon you.

I long for you to receive it.

So examine your heart. What are you focused on in these last days?

Are you praying?

Are you listening?

Are you watching?

The Day of the Lord should not come as a surprise to those who are Mine.

Seek Me now, while there is still time.[121]

And expect the outpouring.

---

[121] Isaiah 55:6-7

If only I knew then

If only I knew then what I know now.

If I could go back and whisper to the version of me who cried herself to sleep, who was desperate to make sense of the pain, who questioned her worth because of who walked away and what didn't work out,

I'd tell her:

It's all working for your good.

The heartbreak wasn't wasted.

The loneliness wasn't punishment.

The detours, the delays, the shattered plans, the people you thought you couldn't live without,

God was using all of it.

Every ounce. Every moment. Every mess.

I didn't know it then. I couldn't see it.

Back then, I thought silence meant abandonment.

I thought no meant rejection.

I thought the loss meant I failed somehow.

I thought if it was hard, it couldn't be good.

But now I see:

You were doing something deeper in me.

You were letting things fall apart so I'd stop holding them above You.

You were letting me sit in the ache so I could learn to come to You, not just for comfort, but for wholeness.

You let me feel the full weight of surrender not because You're cruel, but because You wanted me free.

I didn't know the idols I clung to were slowly choking the life out of me.

I didn't realize I was mistaking Your protection for punishment.

But You were stripping away everything I depended on so I could learn to depend on You.

And even now... I confess...

There are still moments that hurt.

Moments where I look around and think, This doesn't feel good.

This doesn't look like what I prayed for.

But I know now, it doesn't have to feel good for You to be doing good.

You are mending together every broken piece, even the ones I try to hide.

You don't waste pain. You don't forget promises.

Help me to love You...

Even when it feels like I've lost something precious.

Even when the waiting is long and wearisome.

Even when my heart is raw and my prayers feel unanswered.

Help me to love You for who You are—not just for what I hope You'll do.

Give me faith that's not attached to outcomes.

Give me peace that isn't held hostage by my circumstances.

Give me joy that outlasts the tears.

You've been so patient with me.

You've been so kind.

And even now, You're inviting me to rest not because everything makes sense, but because You are still God, and You are still good.

So no I don't have all the answers.

But I do have this truth:

I have no reason to worry.

Because I've seen Your track record.

Because I know how You write redemption into every story, especially mine.

You've never wasted anything.

You've never left me.

And You're not about to start now.

Tearing Down the Hidden Thrones

"Those who cling to worthless idols turn away from God's love for them" [122]

Lord, there's a quiet grief I carry when I think about how many times I've chosen something or someone else over You.
Not because I said You weren't enough— But because my life said it for me.
Idolatry is subtle.
It sneaks in through what I cling to, what I run to,
what I rely on more than You.
It's the things I reach for when I feel empty.
The people I depend on for worth.
The goals I pursue like they're my salvation.
I've had so many idols, Lord. Some I knew. Some I didn't.
And there are still some You have to reveal to me again and again.
Because the temptation to exalt things—even good things—above You... it's real.
You told me in Your word: Put to death, therefore, whatever belongs to your earthly nature... greed, which is idolatry. [123]

---

[122] Jonah 2:8

[123] Colossians 3:5

I've made time for everything but You, Lord.
I've listened to culture and comfort more than Your Spirit.
I've chased affirmation and attention more than Your presence.
I've liked the idea of You, but I still wanted to sit on the throne
of my own life.

I've said, "I don't worship these things," but the truth is,
worship is about what I trust, what I adore, what I give myself
to.
And so often, I've given myself to things that could never carry
me.
Reveal where my trust really lives.
Lord, forgive me.

You've shown me that anything I put in Your place is an idol, even
if I try to disguise it in spiritual language.

You are a jealous God, not in weakness, but in holiness.
You love me too much to let me settle for less than You.
You want my whole heart because You know every idol I turn to
will eventually turn on me.

But still, Lord... sometimes I wrestle.
Sometimes I want to negotiate what I am allowed to touch.
Sometimes I delay obedience while convincing myself I'm still close
to You.

But if You say You want something from me, then I surrender it.
If You say it's in the way, I want it gone.
Because You're not trying to hurt me... You're trying to *heal* me.
You want to be my first instinct.
My first call.
My true foundation.

You reminded me even in the smallest things like how our family
dog waits, patiently watching, fully expecting to receive.
That's the posture You want from me: faith that waits, not
because of what You give but because I know who You are and
that You will provide. [124]
And God, You've been so patient.
You've given me time to grow.
You've held back judgment.
You've shown mercy when I chose convenience over covenant.

So now, I ask You...
Keep my heart soft. Keep my eyes open.
Reveal any idol I've made room for, no matter how hidden or
disguised.
Whether it's a relationship, an image, a goal, a ministry, an idea, or
a fear, if it sits where only You should sit, Lord, tear it down.

---

[124] Genesis 22:14

I don't want to look like I care about You and still keep You at a distance.

I don't want to debate You. I don't want to delay You.

I want to obey You.

Let my time, my talk, my thoughts, my life, reflect that You are my God.

Not just in name, but in truth.

Just Want You

Lord, I want You.
Not just what You give.
Not just the blessings.
Not just the breakthroughs.
I want You.

Because everything I've tried to replace You with has failed me.
You are the only one who satisfies.
You are the answer to my questions.
You are the solution to my deepest problems.
You are the One I was made to worship.

Cleanse my heart. Center my life.
Keep me from the idols that promise fulfillment but deliver only emptiness.

Let my soul declare: Jesus, You alone are Lord.

[Plays Just Want You- Travis Greene ft. Jordan Connell & Chandler Moore]

Hiding in Your Presence

Lord, sometimes I don't even realize I'm hiding.
I just feel tired. I go quiet. I pull away.
I convince myself I'm just processing, or resting, or needing
space—but You know the truth. I'm hiding.

Not hiding from You.
Just hiding in You.
Because the world is loud and heavy, and I am small and weary.
And sometimes I just don't want to be seen by anyone but You.

I've hidden in other things before—
Distractions.
Numbness.
Performance.

I've tried to outrun my emotions and over-explain my fears to
people who could never hold them. But You... You don't demand that
I be okay.
You invite me to come closer, especially when I'm not.
Your presence is the only hiding place that doesn't make me feel
lost.

When I'm in You, I'm not invisible... I'm safe.
I'm not forgotten... I'm held.

I'm not escaping life... I'm anchoring my soul to the only One who gives it.

You said in Your Word: *"He who dwells in the secret place of the Most High shall abide under the shadow of the Almighty."*[125]

Lord, thank You for the shadow. Thank You for the covering. Thank You that I can lay down what I'm carrying—every anxious thought, every buried fear, every ache I can't find the words for—and just be with You.

Sometimes, this is all I can do: sit in Your presence and breathe.

No big declarations.
No powerful prayers.
No polished faith.

Just me.
Just You.
And a quiet trust that You are working, even when I'm too tired to move.

You are my refuge, not because You change all my circumstances... but because You meet me inside of them.

---

[125] Psalm 91:1

You don't tell me to get it together. You hold me together.
You don't wait for me to stand strong. You sit with me when I'm weak.

And Lord... I'm learning not to be ashamed of needing to hide. Because You're not disappointed in my need for You—you delight in being the One I run to.

So here I am.
No more hiding in my thoughts.
No more hiding behind busyness.
No more hiding behind spiritual language when what I really need is stillness.

I'm choosing today to hide in Your presence.
To come away with You.
To be wrapped up in You.
To let Your voice quiet the noise and Your nearness settle the storm in me.

You are my hiding place.
And in You, I am found.

You Remain

Lord...
You had so many reasons to leave me. So many.
All the times I ignored You.
All the ways I doubted You.
When I searched for meaning in everything but You—
When I gave my trust to things that couldn't save me.
I remember when I believed in evil eyes to protect me,
crystals to align me,
ancestors to guide me.
I believed that Florida water could cleanse me and make me new...
when all along, it was only You who could do that.
It was only You who already had.

I called it spirituality... but I was spiritually starving.
I was looking for power in dead things,
seeking truth from places that had none.
I honored creation over the Creator,
thinking I was awakening when I was really drifting further into
darkness.

But even then...
You didn't turn away.
When I was a nonbeliever, You believed in what I could become.
You saw me in my confusion and didn't condemn me—you called me.

You watched me reach for empty rituals,
yet You remained ready to rescue me with real redemption.
And now, Lord, even after coming to know You—
I still fall short.
I still battle old habits, old thinking.
I still try to fix things in my own strength before running to
You.
But You... You don't change.
You don't flinch.
You don't give up.
You remain.[126]
You stayed through the rebellion.
You stayed through the deception.
You stayed through the shame, the cycles, the sins, and the
searching.
You stayed when I was lost in counterfeit light.
And You're still here now, helping me walk in true light.
You have been my consistent grace.
I've watched people walk away for far less.
I've walked away from myself at times.
But not once did You leave.

Lord, I'm overwhelmed by Your mercy.

---

[126] Timothy 2:13

You could've let me stay in bondage.
You could've turned Your back while I turned mine.
But instead, You waited. You loved. You remained.
And now, my heart has only one desire:
To remain in You.

Thank You for staying.
Thank You for revealing Yourself.
Thank You for trading my confusion for clarity,
my darkness for light,
my idols for intimacy,
and my shame for sonship.
You were the only One who could make me new—
and You still are.
I don't ever want to go back.
Not when I've tasted this freedom.
Not when I've seen who You really are.
Jesus, You are the One who never left me.
And now, I never want to leave You.

More Grace to Give

Why do you rush away so quickly?
I see you trying to be faithful
trying to show up, trying to say the right things,
trying to do the right things,
but your heart... your heart still feels hurried.
You enter My presence like someone glancing at a clock.
But I didn't call you here to be efficient.
I called you here to be embraced.
You come to Me hungry, but you leave too soon.
You kneel at My feet but stand before I can finish healing
what's broken.
You bring Me your burdens,
but you pick them up again before I can fully lift them off your
shoulders.
Don't go so quickly.
I wasn't done yet.
I wasn't finished pouring out My peace.
I hadn't yet shown you the depths of My love for you, not just
the world.
I still had more to say,
more to reveal,
more to heal.

You prayed for more of Me,
but then you moved on before I could give you all My grace.

My grace is not one layer thick, it goes deep.

It saturates.

It restores.

It transforms.

There are some things you've been asking for,

wisdom, strength, freedom

but they're not found in striving.

They're found in staying.

Stay with Me longer.

Don't treat our moments like transactions.

You are not a project I want to fix.

You are my child I delight to be with.

Let Me love you slowly.

Let Me pour Myself into the empty places, the ones you rush past.

Let Me interrupt your schedule so I can give you something better than productivity...

—Presence.

Some of the things you've been running after are only found when you're still.

Some of the healing you're desperate for will only come when you stop trying to hurry it.

Some of the answers you're searching for will come while you're simply resting with Me.

So sit with Me.

Breathe with Me.

Let time fall away for just a little while.

I'm not just after your prayer list.

I'm after you.

Don't go so quickly.

Stay a little longer.

I still have more grace to give.[127]

---

[127] James 4:6

Stay

You wonder why sometimes you feel Me so strongly, and other
times I feel far.
But I have not moved. I have not changed.
I am the same yesterday, today, and forever.[128]

Sometimes, you sense Me in the song,
in the tears, in the stillness.
Other times, I seem quiet,
but I'm still there.
I've always been there.
You don't have to feel Me to know that I'm faithful.
I don't fade in and out like the sun behind clouds.
I am not a God who hides to punish, I draw near to refine.

And even when your heart feels dry, your prayers feel flat, and
the heavens feel silent, I am with you.[129]

Don't let praying wear you out.
Prayer is not a performance.
It's not a test you have to pass.
It's not a place to prove how spiritual you are.
It's communion. It's honesty. It's exhale.

---

[128] Hebrews 13:8
[129] Matthew 28:20

Let your prayers be messy.
Let them be wordless. Let them be weary.
I hear them all.[130]

Why do you give yourself so much trouble, My child?
Why do you measure your faith by how you feel, instead of who I
am?
I don't love you more when you cry harder.
I don't listen better when you speak louder.
I'm not impressed by your striving.
I'm moved by your surrender.
Come to Me like a child again.
Tired. Trusting. Needing nothing but My arms.
Let Me carry what you keep trying to fix.[131]
Let Me love you even when your heart feels numb.

Let Me remind you:
My nearness is not a feeling, it's a truth.
You may feel Me more one day, less the next.
But I never change.
And I never leave.

---

[130] Psalm 34:17, 1 John 5:14, Jeremiah 29:12
[131] 1 Peter 5:7

So stay close.

Even if you feel far—stay.

Even if you're tired—stay.

Even when your words run dry—stay.

Because I'm still here.

And I always will be.[132]

_____

[132] Matthew 28:20

Get out of yourself

When you see something broken in those who lead,
when you notice weakness in the ones who are supposed to be
strong
don't rush to judge. Rush to pray.

Yes, there are things that grieve your spirit.
Yes, you long for holiness and truth.
But don't let what you see in others harden your heart in pride or
stir your tongue to gossip.

Ask yourself, have I prayed for them?[133]

Before you speak.
Before you post.
Before you vent.
Have you interceded?[134]

It's easy to criticize from a distance.
It's easy to forget that My priests are human and that My
shepherds are still sheep.

---

[133] 1 Thessalonians 5:11
[134] 1 Timothy 2:1-2

It's easy to forget that those in front are often fighting battles you don't see. You are called to bare one another's burdens. [135]

Yes, I see what you see. In fact, I see even more.
But I didn't call you to become a judge, I called you to become a vessel.

Get out of yourself.
Out of your opinions.
Out of your outrage.
Out of your disappointment long enough to lift up a holy cry instead of a hollow complaint.

You grieve over what's missing,
so ask Me to restore it.
You weep over what's broken,
so stand in the gap [136] and plead for healing.
You ache for purity,
so pray that I purify them.

If I put it on your heart to see it,

_____

[135] Galatians 6:2
[136] Ezekiel 22:30

it may be because I trust you to carry it in prayer, not spread it in pride.

This is the way of love:
to speak less and intercede more.
To call out to Me before calling out others.
To care more about healing than being heard.

So the next time you see something that disturbs you, don't just speak about it.
Speak to Me about it.

Get out of yourself and into My heart.

Not Just Your Strengths

I don't just want your strengths.

I take your shortcomings too.

I welcome your stumbles, your imperfections, your failed attempts to get it right. Because I see beyond them.

I see the yes that lives underneath your struggle.

I see the effort, the way you try again,

the way your heart leans toward Me even when you feel like you're falling short. You don't have to impress Me.

You don't have to earn your place.

I take delight in your desire,

even when your follow-through feels weak.

What matters is that you're not hiding anymore.

Give Me your goodness, yes. But give Me your gaps too.

Give Me your praise and your pain.

Give Me your moments of clarity and your confusion.

Give Me your strength and your trembling.

I want all of you.

I didn't die for the best version of you.

I died for you.[137]

As you are. Right now.

So don't hold back.

Don't retreat when you feel like you've failed.

Come closer. Come completely.

---

[137] Romans 5:8

Because I won't turn you away.

I won't reject what you offer, no matter how small or broken it feels.

I'll take it.

I'll fill it.

I'll make it holy.

Just give Me everything.

Why Me, Lord?

God... why me?
Why do You keep showing up like this?
Why do You keep speaking to me so kindly, so intimately?
You know I'm not the most faithful.
You know how inconsistent I am,
how easily distracted, how slow to obey, how quick to wander I can be.

You know how many times I've questioned, doubted, retreated,
tried to handle life on my own. You know I don't deserve this kind
of nearness...
not this kind of mercy.
So why me?

Why do You still speak? Why do You still pursue?
There are people more disciplined, more holy, more prayerful—
why would You reveal Yourself to someone like me?
Is it pity? Is it just grace?
Is it because I'm broken and You can't resist broken things?
Part of me wants to hide from You because I know I'm
unworthy.

And yet, the deepest part of me aches to stay close
because something in me believes You love me still.
But... why?

Don't be afraid.

You're right, others will look at you and wonder why I speak to you like this. They'll wonder why I use you, why I dwell so close, why I whisper such depth into your heart.

They'll say, "It's not because she's righteous." And they'll be right. It's not because you've earned it.

It's not because you prayed long enough, performed well enough, or proved yourself worthy.

It's because I'm good.

It's because I'm compassionate.

It's because I choose to be close to the ones who need Me most.

I speak to you not because you deserve it,

but because My heart longs to.

Because My mercy moves Me.

Because My love compels Me.

This is who I am:

I am drawn to your weakness.

I am stirred by your hunger.

I am moved by the ache in your cry.

And even when your hands are empty,

I see that your heart is open.

So no, this isn't about what you've done.

It's about what I want to do.

In you. Through you. With you.

I speak because I love you.

I reveal Myself because it brings Me joy.

And I won't stop,

not because of who you are, but because of who I am.

I will keep coming.

I will keep speaking.

Because My heart just can't stay silent.[138]

_____

[138] Psalm 84:11

Call to Buoyancy

My child, I want you to rise above the storm and see what I see. The earth was once formless and dark, but My Spirit hovered over the waters.[139] Likewise, I am calling you into the deep to learn how to remain over the waters, not to be overtaken by them.

You know how to swim. You've felt the push and pull of the waves, how they move you even when you think you're in control. You've entered the water directly in front of your place of safety, only to look up and realize you've drifted far from where you began. That's what the deep does it carries you further than you intended, often before you even realize it.

When the waters get too deep and you feel yourself going under, remember to keep calm, and float. Do not panic, for panic will weigh you down.
Now imagine this in the midst of a storm, darkness, raging waters, violent waves. Many would be weighed down by desperation. But I want you to learn to ride the storm, for I am intentionally calling you into the deep.[140]

I showed you a vision of a buoy, a floating object anchored firmly to guide and warn of storms. The buoy is not just afloat on its

---

[139] Genesis1:2
[140] Mark 4:39

own, it is attached to something stable, keeping it anchored even in violent waves. Like the buoy, you must be connected to Me, your anchor, to remain steady.

If you connect to the wrong things, or carry burdens not meant for you, you will be weighed down and unable to withstand the storm. Beware of distractions that pull you from your purpose—I have a plan and a pace. Let My pace set your pace. I went first. I go first. Walk in step with Me.

I do not want you weighed down by things you were never graced to carry. Discern the storms and locations I have assigned you. Do not waste time in battles not yours. I will grace you to weather the storms I call you to, but I am not obligated to grace you for others' storms.

Remember Nehemiah, who said, "I am doing a great work, so I cannot come."[141] Like him, be determined, aware, and focused on your assignment. Do not be intimidated by opposition or distractions. I ask you, why run from the storm? Am I not the

---

[141] Nehemiah 6:3

Creator and Controller of the oceans?[142] Be patient, wait on Me[143], be brave and courageous[144]. Let Me do the moving.

Waiting exposes idols and false coping, —let it bring you to Me.

I showed you the story of the axe head lost in the Jordan River[145], the piece of wood that made it float again represents Me, Christ. I raise you from the depths, from under the weight of sin and despair, and place you above the storm and underneath the weight of My glory. So rise up. Reclaim your usefulness. Get back to the work I have for you. I want you above the storm, carrying the weight of My glory, not the burdens of the world.

The buoy doesn't just float, it watches. It listens. It senses. It speaks.
Buoys are equipped with sensors to detect changes in the environment—atmospheric pressure, wave height, ocean currents, wind speeds. When a storm is coming, a buoy knows before it hits. And it does not keep this knowledge to itself.
It sends a signal.

---

[142] Psalm 107:29, Psalm 95:5, Genesis 1:9-10

[143] Psalm 27:14

[144] Joshua 1:9

[145] 2 Kings 6:1-7.

Even in isolation, a buoy is never alone.

It's part of a network. A system of communication that allows others to be warned, positioned, and prepared. When one detects danger, the message travels, and others respond. Likewise, I have not only called you to stand, but to signal. You are part of something bigger than yourself.

I've placed My Spirit in you not only to anchor you, but to give you discernment. You will feel the pressure shift before the storm shows itself. You'll sense what others miss. That sensitivity is not a burden—it's a gift. Use it.

But hear Me: the buoy cannot fulfill its purpose without power. It must remain connected—not only to its anchor, but to its source. Some are solar powered, charged by what they receive from above. So are you. You need continual exposure to Me—My Word, My presence, My light—to remain alert and active.

And My child, communication between buoys doesn't happen through striving—it's automatic when they're in the right position and properly charged.

You don't have to force connection with others I've anchored near you.

When you are both aligned with Me, your signals will reach one another.

Community in My kingdom is not accidental. It is divinely placed, intentionally connected, and mutually strengthening.
Just as buoys are strategically deployed along coasts, harbors, and in the open sea, I've strategically placed you—not for comfort, but for purpose.
You are not where you are by accident. Your very presence is a warning to some, a comfort to others, and a reminder to all that the storm will pass, and that I am present even in its midst.

So when the winds start to howl, and you feel the rise in pressure, do not grow anxious. Lift your eyes. Stay connected to your Source.
Send the signal.
And trust that I have placed others around you to do the same.

There is a holy rhythm in My Body. When one suffers, all feel it.
When one stands, others are strengthened.
This is how My Church, like My buoys, rides the storm together.

You are not alone in the water.
You are anchored, alert, and assigned.
Let the storm come. Let it rage.
You know who holds the seas.

The Tension Between Grace and Truth

Lord, I'm sitting with the tension in these chapters.

In 1 Corinthians 4, Paul says not to pass judgment before the appointed time which reminds me that You alone know the motives of every heart. He models humility, surrender, and the posture of a servant who answers to You alone.[146] Then in chapter 5, he speaks boldly and firmly about confronting sin in the church, calling for a cleansing, a correction, a line to be drawn.[147]

At first glance, these feel like opposite instructions:
don't judge yet confront.
Stay humble yet take action.
But the more I read, the more I hear the wisdom in the balance.
You are not calling me to be self-righteous or harsh.
You are not asking me to take Your seat as Judge,
but You are asking me to care enough to tell the truth in love,
and to guard what is sacred.

I don't want to be the kind of believer who excuses sin in the name of grace, or who becomes arrogant and self-righteous in the name of truth. Lord, teach me how to discern rightly with Your heart.

---

[146] 1 Corinthians 4

[147] 1 Corinthians 5

I'm teaching you the difference between correction and condemnation, between spiritual discernment and fleshly judgment.[148] What I desire is a heart that loves righteousness because it loves Me. One that speaks truth, not to tear down, but to restore. Don't forget I oppose the proud [149] even when they are right. But I give grace to the humble, even when they're in the process of learning.

Your job is not to expose for exposure's sake, but to protect the purity of My people beginning with your own heart. Walk gently. Walk boldly.
Walk in step with Me, and I will give you the words, the timing, and the love that reflects My character.

_____

[148] Romans 8:1

[149] James 4:6, 1 Peter 5:5

The Slow Work of Compassion

Lord, I'm starting to notice this slow, quiet work You're doing in me. My reactions aren't always as quick to judge as they once were. I'm feeling things I used to brush off.

My heart softens in places where it used to harden.

I recognize now that this is You. You're stretching my heart. Teaching me how to carry compassion, not just as a feeling, but as a posture. It's uncomfortable sometimes. I still resist. I still want to pull back into what's safe and familiar, into assumptions, into self-protection. But You're making it harder to ignore the pain in others. Harder to scroll past. Harder to dismiss.

I'm forming My heart in you.[150] Compassion is not weakness; it's My strength flowing through your surrender.[151] I'm teaching you to see people the way I do, to love not by instinct but by revelation. You prayed to be more like Me. This is the answer.

Not always in grand gestures, but in the hidden choice to pause. To care. To listen. To forgive. You are growing in grace, don't rush it. Keep leaning in, and I'll keep making room in you for more of My heart.

---

[150] Psalm 103:8 , Psalm 145:8-9

[151] Colossians 3:12

Every crack in your heart is a place where I can pour my grace.[152]

_____

[152] Psalm 147:3

A Heart in Progress

God, here I am again.
Torn between what I know and what I still struggle to live.

I love You, I really do but sometimes, I'm ashamed of how easily
I drift, how quickly I react. I thought I'd be further along by
now.
More patient. More consistent.
Less defensive. Less insecure.

I get discouraged because I teach about surrender, but I still
hold onto control. I pray for a pure heart, but sometimes I feed
and entertain the very things that stain it.

I long to be whole, but if I'm honest, I still nurse some
brokenness like it's familiar comfort at times.
I compare. I get bitter. I doubt. I overthink.

And still... I want You.
Not just Your help or Your blessings.
I want You to be close, to be known by You, to be changed by
You.

I don't know how to always get it right, but I'm trying to stop
hiding when I get it wrong.

Because I know You don't require perfection to meet me.
You only ask for honesty. And this is mine.

I'm in progress, God. Not perfect. Not pretending. Just in process.
Still being made. Still being shaped, but You know this. And I trust
You won't give up on me.

Disappointed?

Lord, sometimes I feel like I've let You down.
When I miss the mark. When I procrastinate. When I shrink back.
When I know what You've asked of me, and I still hesitate or worse, ignore it.

I carry this weight sometimes... like I've disappointed You.
Like I've wasted too much time. Missed too many moments.

There are days when I feel like I've cost myself something I can't get back.
Opportunities. Growth. Intimacy. Obedience.

And under it all is this quiet, nagging fear of what if You're disappointed in me?

I want to please You, not just because You're God, but because You're good.

Because You've been so patient with me.
Because You believed in me when I didn't.
Because I never want to be careless with Your grace.
But God... sometimes I still mess it up.

And that fear creeps in saying "You've failed Him."

Child, how can you disappoint the One who knew your entire story before you lived a single day of it?[153]

I chose you knowing every detour, every delay, every moment of doubt.
I am not surprised by your stumbles.
I am not fragile. I do not love you because of your flawless performance.
I love you because I made you, redeemed you, and called you Mine [154].

Disappointment belongs to those who had unrealistic expectations.
I don't operate like that.
I am the Alpha and the Omega. [155]
I knew the beginning, the middle, and the mess...
and I still said yes to you.

What you call failure, I often call formation.
What you see as delay, I see as preparation.
You have not ruined what I've spoken over you.

_____

[153] Ephesians 1:4

[154] Ephesians 2:10

[155] Revelation 1:8

So, get up, not to earn My love, but because you're already held by it.

Walk with Me. You're not behind. You're not disqualified.

I'm still writing the story, trust the Author.

I direct your steps. I delight in every detail of your lives. Though you stumble, you will never fall, for I hold you by the hand. [156]

---

[156] Psalm 37:23-24

What Frustration Revealed

God, I've been sitting with this question...
What did the last situation that frustrated me really reveal
about my heart?

Because it wasn't just about what happened.
It was how quickly I reacted. How deep it cut. How long it
lingered.
I thought I was past certain triggers, but they still pull things
up.
I thought I was more surrendered in that area, but I felt the
tug to control. I thought I trusted You more, but truthfully,
I got anxious, offended, resentful.

It showed me that my heart still has places where pride hides.
Where fear whispers. Where expectations become silent demands.
It showed me that sometimes I care more about being right
than being righteous. That I still wrestle with being seen, heard,
validated. That I do not like when things feel out of my hands—
even though I keep saying they are in Yours.

I do not like what it revealed... but I want to bring it to You
instead of pretending it is not there.

What frustrates you often points to what still needs healing.

Not because I am mad at you because I love you enough to show you where I am working. Let the frustration be a window, not a wall. Let it lead you into truth, not shame. I am not afraid of what surfaces when life presses you. I am refining it. I am refining you.[157]

Come closer. I will show you how to respond differently next time. I will show you what freedom looks like. Let Me hold the part of your heart that still tightens up when you do not feel in control. Let Me speak peace into the parts that still flare up when you feel overlooked or misunderstood.

I am not exposing your heart to condemn you.
I am revealing it so I can heal you.

---

[157] James 1:2-4

Keep Me Close and Keep Me Low.

Father,

Forgive me for the times I have moved ahead of You,

assuming I knew what You would say,

assuming I understood the full picture,

assuming I did not need to ask again.

Keep me from the arrogance of familiarity.

Do not let me confuse past experience with present direction.

Teach me to seek You fresh each day, each step, each decision.

Let my instinct be to check with You first,

not after things fall apart, but before I take a step.

I do not want to operate out of my own wisdom, my own

patterns, or my own reasoning. I want to move in rhythm with

You.

You are not a system to figure out or a formula to predict,

You are the Living God, and I never want to treat Your presence

casually.

So keep me close and keep me low.

Let my confidence come from communion with You not from

assumptions.

I surrender my tendency to lead myself.
Lead me instead.

In Jesus name, Amen.

Are You there God?

Lord,

Sometimes I panic when I don't feel You.

When I don't hear You like I did before.

When I don't cry in worship like I used to.

When the Scriptures feel more like study than revelation.

And in the quiet, I worry if You've left me.

I know Your Word says that You'll never leave me nor forsake me.

But honestly, sometimes it feels like You did.

And I hate that my faith still depends so much on feelings.

I should know better by now.

I should be more mature than this.

But here I am searching, aching, fearing,

Just wanting to know that You're still here.

I miss the warmth, the weight, the whisper.

I miss the nearness that used to undo me.

My beloved, I am right here.

Your tears do not summon Me,

and your dry spells do not repel Me.

I am not fragile like that. I am not emotional like man.[158]

I AM Presence even when you feel absence.

---

[158] Hebrews 4:15

The truth is, I'm teaching you how to walk by faith, not by feeling [159].

I'm growing roots beneath the surface,

building trust that doesn't rely on goosebumps or good days.

You want the fire, but sometimes I lead you through fog,

not to confuse you,

but to train your ears to hear My voice when nothing else makes sense.

If I died to get to you, what could make Me walk away now?

Nothing.

Pray like you are being heard because you are.

even when you do not feel Me, I am still faithful.

---

[159] 2 Corinthians 5:7

False God

Idolatry is not always carved in stone.

It does not always come with a name like Baal or golden calves.

Sometimes it looks like a version of Me.

a version shaped by your preferences,

your comfort,

your expectations.

But I will not compete with a counterfeit of Myself.

You grieve over idols of the world,

technology, success, self, fame—

and you are right to be watchful.

But I want to show you the subtler ones:

- The god who always agrees with you.
- The god who only blesses and never disciplines.
- The god who promises ease, not endurance.
- The god who speaks only through emotion, never through silence.

That is not Me. [60]

I am not made in your image. You are made in Mine.

And when you worship who you want Me to be instead of who I am,

you build an altar to something that cannot save you.

----

[60] 1 Corinthians 8:4

Even your idea of "feeling My presence" can become an idol,
when it matters more to you than My truth.
I love to reveal Myself to you,
but I will not be reduced to a sensation.
I came to dwell in your spirit, not just your senses.
I correct because I love. I stay silent to strengthen your hearing.
I say "no" sometimes because I see beyond now.
And I do not answer every prayer the way you hope,
because I am too good to give you less than My will.

So tear down every image
you have built from disappointment, delay, or desire.
Come to Me as I am.
Let My Word define Me.
Let My Spirit reveal Me.
You will find that I am more faithful than you imagined.
More just than you expected.[161]
More holy than you understood.
And more loving than you deserve.
But I will not share My throne,[162]
not even with a false version of Myself.

_____

[161] Ephesians 3:20

[162] Exodus 20:3, Isaiah 45:5, Exodus 34:14

Autocorrect

Lord, I've noticed something about myself lately.

I have this leaning toward what needs to be fixed,

what needs to be exposed, what needs to be made right.

My heart burns for truth.

I am quick to correct.

I spot the error and want to fix it—

almost instinctively.

Like autocorrect:

automatic, immediate, and often uninvited.

Sometimes it comes from a place of care,

sometimes from conviction.

But if I am honest...

Sometimes it comes from pride.

Sometimes out of fear.

Fear that compromise will creep in,

that reverence will be lost,

that we'll forget who You really are.

I've tried to protect Your truth...

but I haven't always protected Your heart in the process.

I've spoken with boldness,

but not always with love.

I've leaned into righteousness,

but sometimes away from mercy.

I've tried to guard Your truth with clenched fists
instead of open hands.
And in doing so,
I think I may have silenced the softness
that makes Your voice so irresistible.

And all the while,
You have been the One autocorrecting me.
You have been editing my assumptions,
highlighting the tone behind my words,
undoing the parts of me that try to be the editor
instead of the image-bearer.
I have been the one constantly being adjusted by Your mercy,
rewritten by Your grace,
and humbled by Your patience.
I want to carry Your truth well, Lord,
but not at the expense of Your heart.
So here I am again Lord, turning inward,
inviting Your correction.
not wanting to miss my log
while I am busy spotting the speck.[63]

I see your zeal. I see the ache in you for what is holy. And I
honor that.

_____

[63] Matthew 7:3-5, Luke 6:41-42

But be careful, truth without tenderness can cut more than it heals.[164]

Correction without compassion can sound like condemnation.[165]

Yes, I correct.

Yes, I discipline.[166]

But My kindness is what leads hearts to repentance.[167]

not your clarity, not your boldness, not your insight.

You do not have to choose between love and truth.

I am both.

And when you speak on My behalf, you must carry both together.

Not watered down. Not weaponized.

But wrapped in grace that reminds people they are still welcome at the table.

I did not just flip tables[168], I washed feet[169].

I did not just confront, I called close.

Do not forget that.

So lead, but let Me lead you first.

Let correction flow from communion.

---

[164] Ephesians 4:15

[165] Romans 8:1, John 3:17

[166] Proverbs 3:11-12

[167] Revelation 3:19

[168] Matthew 21:12-13, Mark 11:15-17, John 2:13-16

[169] John 12:3-5, 12-17

Let conviction be carried on compassion.

Let your words be soaked in My presence before they are ever spoken.

I do not need defenders.

I need image-bearers.[170]

Let your life speak before your lips do.

Let love open the door before truth walks in.

That is how they will know Me.

And that is how they will know you walk with Me.[171]

---

[170] Genesis 1:26-27

[171] John 13:35, Micah 6:8

After the Mask Drops

Lord, You've freed me from the need to perform for You.
You have broken that lie that said I had to earn my place in Your
presence.
With You, I can be bare.
Broken.
In process.
But what I am still learning... is how to live that way with people.
Because the narrow way is hard.
Not just because it costs me something,
but because I am afraid of what it will cost in how I am seen.
Will they still honor me if I'm honest about my weaknesses?
Will they still follow me if I stop pretending to always be strong?
Will they offer me the same grace I've received from You?
Or will their perception change?
Will their acceptance withdraw?
Will their approval fade?

Sometimes it feels safer to collapse in Your arms
than to stand imperfect in front of theirs.
I know I am not called to perform.
But I still fear the silence in the room when I stop performing.
I still brace myself for judgment when I stop hiding.
I still ache for belonging in spaces that make me feel I must
earn it.

And I hate that it still matters so much to me.
But here I am, again.
With trembling hands and a heart that longs to be free—
not just with You,
but in front of them too.

You were never meant to carry their expectations like chains.[172]
Let go. I did not set you apart to fit in.
I set you apart to reflect Me.[173]
The grace I have given you is not fragile.
It does not vanish in the face of imperfection.
It covers. It restores. It frees.
And when others cannot see you clearly, I still do.
When they measure your worth by appearances or strength,
remember, I chose you in your weakness.
You are not here to impress them.
You are here to walk with Me.
Some will misunderstand.
Some will walk away.
But the ones I have assigned to your life,
they will recognize My Spirit in you, even when you are undone.

---

[172] Matthew 11:28-30

[173] Jeremiah 1:5

Let them see you becoming.

That is where My glory shines.

So no, the narrow way is not easy[174],

but I walk it with you.

And every step you take in truth

is a step further into freedom.

_____

[174] Matthew 7:13-14, Luke 9:23, Matthew 16:24, 2 Timothy 3:12

Your Turn

So now, I place this book in your hands not as a conclusion,
but as a beginning.
Because *Pen'd in His Presence* is an invitation.
And once you've stepped through, you can't unknow the nearness of God.
You can't un-hear the whisper that found you in the dark.
You can't un-feel the gentle weight of His love resting on your soul.
If these words have stirred anything in you, grief, hope, longing, conviction
then let them lead you deeper.
Not into emotion for its own sake,
but into *communion* with the One who waits to meet you in the secret place.
Do not just read-respond.
Do not just remember-return.
Return to stillness.
Return to honesty.
Return to the voice of the One who sees you and still draws near.
There is more He wants to say.
Not just to me,
but to *you*.
So take up your own pen.
Let it tremble if it must.

Let it run out of ink, if that is what it takes.

But do not stop writing.

Do not stop listening.

He is still speaking.

His presence is the safest, truest, and most sacred place you will ever be.

Declarations: Anchored in God's Word. Transformed by His Love.

- I am loved with an unconditional love that is always available and never dependent on my actions. -(Romans 5:8)

- God's love heals the broken places in my heart and makes me whole again. I embrace the healing power of God's love, allowing it to restore every broken area of my heart. I surrender my wounds to God. - (Psalm 147:3)

- I am deeply loved by God, and His love is enough to satisfy every longing of my heart. I am fully satisfied in God's love, knowing that His love is all I need to fulfill the deepest desires of my heart. - (Psalm 42:1)

- I am secure in my identity, rooted in God's unshakable love for me. - (Romans 8:38-39)

- I am always in God's presence, and His love is a constant source of peace and joy in my life. I rest in the unbroken presence of God. -(Psalm 145:18)

- Hope arises in my heart because God's love has never failed and will never fail me. God's love is unshakable and will always carry me through every trial and circumstance. I find my safety and peace in God's loving arms. - (Lamentations 3:22-23)

- I live each day with purpose, knowing that my life is meant to reflect the love of God and bring glory to His name. - (Ephesians 2:10)

- I will worship God not out of duty, but as a response to His boundless love for me. My worship today flows naturally from the overwhelming love I experience in God's presence. - (Psalm 9:1)

- Love is not just a feeling but an action, and I choose to live out God's love in tangible ways. I choose to live with a deep love for others, a heart of forgiveness, and a boldness that comes from knowing I am deeply loved by God. - (1 John 3:18)

- I am a recipient of God's radical grace, and I extend that same grace to others. -(Ephesians 4:32)

- Forgiveness is the key to freedom, and I choose to forgive as I have been forgiven. I choose to forgive, releasing others and myself, and embracing the freedom that comes from God's love and forgiveness. - (Colossians 3:13)

- I am continually transformed by God's love, becoming more like Him as His love shapes every thought, word, and action. Transforming me from the inside out, shaping my thoughts, actions, and identity. - (2 Corinthians 3:18)

- I am worthy of God's love, and I am learning to receive it fully, without reservation. I open my heart to fully receive God's love, accepting my worth as He sees me—perfectly loved and chosen. - (1 John 3:1)

- I am a living part of God's magnificent love story, experiencing His love for me every day. - (Ephesians 2:10)

- In the presence of God's love, fear has no place. I choose courage over fear. I walk boldly in God's love, knowing that fear is banished by His perfect love, and I choose courage in all things. - (1 John 4:18)

- I surrender my own plans and trust in God's perfect purpose for my life. I release my control and trust that God's love is guiding me toward His perfect purpose for my life. - (Proverbs 3:5-6)

Author Testimony

She was not looking for God...but God was looking for her

To help you understand my story, I want to share the story of a woman named Mary Magdalene with you. You can find her story throughout the Gospels but what always stands out to me is how Jesus met her right where she was. The Bible tells us that Mary had been bound by darkness and tormented by seven demons.[175] Her life was marked by bondage, brokenness, and rejection. But when Jesus showed up, everything changed. Mary was not out searching for a Savior, but her Savior came searching for her. And when He found her, He did not shame her. He did not remind her of her past. He freed her. He restored her. He gave her identity, dignity, and purpose. And if you keep reading, you will see that Mary became one of Jesus' most devoted followers. The very first person He appeared to after His resurrection.[176]

Just like Mary, I have known what it feels like to be bound. To be stuck in cycles of darkness, rejection, and self-inflicted suffering. I have known what it feels like to be searching for a way out only to have Jesus find me instead. I was bound by generational chains that led me down dark, destructive paths.

---

[175] Luke 8:2, Mark 16:9

[176] Matthew 28:1-10, Mark 16:1-11, John 20:1-18

Alcoholism, addiction, same sex attraction, witchcraft, sexual sin and so much more. I experienced abuse physical, emotional, and mental. But that was not all. I carried heartbreak, insecurity, disappointment, rejection, and shame like they were stitched into my identity.

I carried all of it, hidden beneath accomplishments, laughter, and a carefully crafted mask. But inside... I was completely empty. I carried burdens I was never built to bear. I became self-reliant, hardened, leaning only on my own understanding. I did not know God, I was not raised in church, and I surely did not believe He could hear me. I let the world convince me that because of my choices, God wanted nothing to do with me. I was too far gone and that I had already disqualified myself.

But can I tell you the truth? That is a lie.
A lie straight from hell, designed to keep us from the only One who can truly heal, love, redeem, and restore us. Ephesians 2:4-5 reminds us: "But because of His great love for us, God, who is rich in mercy, made us alive with Christ even when we were dead in transgressions."[177]

And the same God who came looking for Mary Magdalene came looking for me. It did not start in a church or with religion. It

---

[177] Ephesians 2:4-5

started alone, in my room, just me, a Bible, and a broken girl desperate for something real. I did not know what to expect, but I opened His Word. I searched for truth. I searched for proof. And little by little, I found answers, and in those answers, I found Him. The way, the truth, the life.[178] The more I read, the more my heart softened. The more I prayed, the more my desires shifted. I did not change myself; I surrendered.

Before I knew it, I was being loosened from the very chains that once had me bound. Not because I tried harder but because Jesus changed me from the inside out. Ephesians 2:8 reminds us, "It is by grace you have been saved, through faith and this is not from yourselves, it is the gift of God."[179]

God took my breaking point and a moment that started with me misinterpreting Isaiah 1. But even in my misunderstanding, He was working. That scripture exposed the lies I had been clinging to – the rituals, the practices, the counterfeit "truths" the world had convinced me were harmless. The new moons, the altars, the spiritual rituals I thought were helping me – God revealed they were nothing but distractions from Him. And in His mercy, He stripped it all away. The lies. The idols. The counterfeit comforts. The veil was torn. Conviction hit me like never before. I dismantled my ancestral altar. I threw out the tarot cards. The

---

[178] John 14:6

[179] Ephesians 2:8

crystals. I got sober. I committed to walking in purity. At first, I was overwhelmed by shame and guilt ashamed of how I had been deceived, broken by how I had misused the very gifts God had given me... But even then - God met me with mercy.

I never set out to change. I never planned to be delivered. But when I encountered the love, the grace, the truth of Jesus... I could not stay the same.

I am not perfect - far from it. But I am free. I am forgiven. I am His.
On April 10th, 2023, I was baptized, surrendering my life to Jesus. Since then, He has redeemed the very gifts I once misused. I pray this serves as proof that not only is God faithful but that He redeems. In Him cycles can be broken, minds can be renewed, hearts can be restored, and faith even faith as small as a mustard seed, can change everything.

If He can do it for me... I promise you; He can do it for you.
Lord, thank You. Without You, I am nothing. I owe it all to You.

INDEX

www.ingramcontent.com/pod-product-compliance
Lightning Source LLC
Chambersburg PA
CBHW060417130626
46555CB00005B/2107